Anonymous, (Mass.) Boston

Dedication of the Monument on Boston Common Erected to the Memory of the Men of Boston who Died in the Civil War

Anonymous, (Mass.) Boston

Dedication of the Monument on Boston Common Erected to the Memory of the Men of Boston who Died in the Civil War

ISBN/EAN: 9783337404802

Printed in Europe, USA, Canada, Australia, Japan

Cover: Foto ©ninafisch / pixelio.de

More available books at **www.hansebooks.com**

DEDICATION

OF THE

Monument on Boston Common

ERECTED TO THE MEMORY

OF

THE MEN OF BOSTON

WHO DIED IN THE CIVIL WAR.

PRELIMINARY ARRANGEMENTS.

HISTORY OF THE MONUMENT. — LAYING THE CORNER-STONE. — ARRANGEMENTS FOR THE DEDICATION.

LIST OF ILLUSTRATIONS.

	PAGE
VIEW OF THE MONUMENT	Frontispiece.

THE STATUES.

AMERICA	43
PEACE	45
THE SAILOR	47
HISTORY	48
THE SOLDIER	51

THE MEZZO-RILIEVOS.

DEPARTURE FOR THE WAR	52
THE SANITARY COMMISSION	53
RETURN FROM THE WAR	54
THE NAVY	55

CONTENTS.

	PAGE
PRELIMINARY ARRANGEMENTS	9–40
HISTORY OF THE MONUMENT	11
Committee Appointed to Consider the Expediency of Erecting a Monument	11
Report of Committee	11
Committee Appointed to Procure Plans and Estimates	13
Committee on Monument of 1870 Appointed	14
List of Competitors	14
Design Accepted	15
Committee on Monument of 1871 Appointed	15
Contract Made with Mr. Milmore	15
LAYING THE CORNER-STONE	16–34
The Procession	16–20
The Chief Marshal and Staff	16
Massachusetts Volunteer Militia	16
The Grand Army of the Republic	17
The Governor, Executive Council, Military Staff, and Escort	20
The Mayor and City Government, and Escort	20
The Grand Lodge F. & A.M. of Massachusetts	20
Boston Fire Department	20
Prayer by Rev. Warren H. Cudworth	21
Hymn by Dexter Smith	22
Address by Alderman Robert Cowdin	23
Address of the Hon. William Gaston	26
Address of the Hon. Charles Levi Woodbury	31
List of Articles Deposited in the Corner-Stone	32
ARRANGEMENTS FOR THE DEDICATION	34–39
Committee on Monument of 1877 Appointed	34
Report of Committee Announcing Completion of Monument	35
Dedication Authorized	36
Chief Marshal's Circular	37
DESCRIPTION OF THE MONUMENT	41–55
General Description	43
List of Articles Deposited under the Column by the City of Boston	45
List of Articles Deposited under the Column by the Grand Army of the Republic	46
List of Articles deposited under the Column by the Military Order of the Loyal Legion	47

CONTENTS.

	PAGE
The Statue of America	49
The Statue of Peace	50
The Statue of the Sailor	50
The Statue of History	51
The Statue of the Soldier	52
The Bas-Rilievo, "Departure for the War"	52
The Bas-Rilievo, "The Sanitary Commission"	53
The Bas-Rilievo, "Return from the War"	54
The Bas-Rilievo, "The Navy"	55
THE PROCESSION	57–87
The Chief Marshal and Staff	60
The Governor and Staff	61
The Massachusetts Volunteer Militia	62
The First Division	63
The Second Division	70
The Third Division	71
The Fourth Division	72
The Fifth Division	75
The Sixth Division	81
The Seventh Division	83
THE DEDICATION	89–139
Prayer of Rev. Warren H. Cudworth	92
Surrender of the Monument by the Sculptor	96
Request to the Masons to Dedicate the Monument	96
Response of the Grand Master	97
Introductory Prayer by Rev. Joshua Young, Grand Chaplain	98
The Consecration	98
Invocation and Prayer of Consecration, by Rev. Alonzo H. Quint, Grand Chaplain	99
Address of the Grand Master, M.W. Percival L. Everett	102
Proclamation by the Grand Marshal	113
Remarks of Alderman Francis Thompson, upon delivering the Monument to the Mayor	113
Remarks of Hon. Frederick O. Prince, Mayor	118
Address of Hon. Charles Devens	126
ILLUMINATIONS AND EVENING CONCERT	141
FINAL PROCEEDINGS OF THE CITY COUNCIL	143
Vote of thanks to the Hon. Charles Devens	143
Vote of thanks to Col. Augustus P. Martin, and Aids	143
Vote of thanks to Commodore Foxhall A. Parker	143

CITY OF BOSTON.

IN BOARD OF ALDERMEN, Oct. 1, 1877.

Ordered, That the Clerk of Committees be requested to prepare and print an account of the ceremonies attending the Dedication of the Army and Navy Monument; and that fifteen hundred copies be printed for the use of the City Government, to be distributed under the direction of the Committee on Printing; the expense to be charged to the appropriation for Incidentals.

IN COMMON COUNCIL, Oct. 4, 1877.

Concurred.

Approved, October 4, 1877.

Press of Rockwell & Churchill, 39 Arch Street, Boston.

HISTORY OF THE MONUMENT.

At a meeting of the Common Council, on the 8th of March, 1866, Mr. Clement Willis offered an order for the appointment of a joint committee, "to take into consideration the expediency of erecting a Monument in the city, in some prominent place, commemorative of the fallen heroes who so heroically aided in putting down the Southern Rebellion, and in sustaining the Constitution of our Country and the Union of the States." The order was passed without opposition, and the President appointed Clement Willis, Jarvis D. Braman, and Benjamin Dean as members of the committee on the part of the Council.

The Board of Aldermen, at a meeting on the 12th of March, concurred in the passage of the order, and Aldermen Samuel D. Crane and J. S. Tyler were joined to the committee.

On the 16th of April, 1866, the committee submitted the following report: —

IN BOARD OF ALDERMEN, April 16, 1866.

The Joint Special Committee appointed to take into consideration the expediency of erecting a Monument, in some prominent place in this city, to commemorate the fallen heroes who aided in putting down the Southern Rebellion, and in sustaining the Constitution of our Country and the Union of the States, beg leave to submit the following report: —

On the 15th day of April, 1861, the President of the United States announced to the country, by proclamation, that seven States of the Union had rebelled against the Government, setting at defiance its authority by force of arms; and he called upon the loyal States for seventy-five thousand men "to maintain the honor, the integrity, and existence of our national union, and the perpetuity of popular government."

The astonishing magnitude which the Rebellion rapidly assumed, and which was not fully comprehended until many months later, necessitated repeated calls upon the country for men, first to organize a great army equal to the emergency, and then to fill the place of those who fell in the desperate struggle of four years which followed.

The noble manner in which Massachusetts responded to the wants of the Government is already recorded in impartial history. The citizens of Boston, without distinction of party, laying aside business in all its various forms, flocked to the standard of their country, determined to die, if need be, in its defence. The young, the middle-aged, and the old men could not be restrained from serving in the defence of their country when the dear-bought liberties achieved by their fathers were in jeopardy. Our city presented for many weeks the activity of a garrisoned town; troops from all parts of New England pressing through it on their way to answer the call of the Chief Executive of the Government, and to defend, from fratricidal hands, the country, of which the peerless Washington was the father.

Many of us, in those trying days, bade adieu, never again to behold in life, the manly forms of brothers, sons, and friends. And to those who fell in the cause of Liberty, Union, and the Constitution, the City of Boston is called upon by the great heart of the people, beating through its public servants, to erect a suitable memento to their memory,— a memory that should ever be kept green in the inmost hearts of the people. To commemorate, therefore, the cause and their achievements, to keep in view an imperishable record of this heroic period, and the services of those who made it, your committee are of the unanimous opinion that a Monument, suitable to the grandeur of the subject, and the proverbial liberality of our citizens, should be erected by the City Council of Boston in some conspicuous place, to be hereafter determined.

Monuments have been erected in other countries to honor the deeds of great warriors, whose skill in arms tended only to fasten the chains of power still stronger upon a too-confiding people; while the deeds of our heroes, whom we propose to honor, caused the chain to fall from four millions of the human race, to whom, and to whose descendants, through the blessings of a Divine Providence, they restored liberty and the attributes of manhood. And not only did they aid in restoring to liberty those upon whom the brand of servitude had been stamped for years, but they not the less emancipated our own Southern brethren from the customs of the past, and placed them in new relations to humanity and progress, where they will be able to enjoy a freedom never before known to them. The committee would respectfully recommend the passage of the accompanying order : —

Ordered, That a committee, consisting of two on the part of the Board of Aldermen, and three on the part of the Common Council, to whom shall be added the President of the Council, be authorized, in consultation with the Mayor, to advertise for plans and estimates for the erection of a Monument in honor of the memory of those citizens of Boston who have fallen in the service of their country during the late Rebellion ; said plans and estimates, with a site for the location of the Monument, to be reported to the City Council, and the expense attending the same to be charged to the appropriation for war expenses.

The order was adopted, and, in accordance with the recommendation, a committee was appointed, consisting of Aldermen Samuel D. Crane and John S. Tyler, Councilmen Joseph Story (President), Clement Willis, Jarvis D. Braman, and Benjamin Dean.

This committee advertised for designs, specifications, and estimates, and offered a premium of three hundred dollars for the design which should receive the approval of the City Council. About thirty designs and models were received from architects and sculptors in different parts of the country. The number and variety of the designs, and the high character of the competition, made the duty of selection one of great difficulty and delicacy ; but the choice of the committee finally fell upon the design submitted by Hammatt Billings, of Boston, and they offered it for acceptance to the City Council. They also recommended "Flagstaff Hill," the highest elevation on Boston Common, as a suitable site for the

Monument. The estimated expense of erecting the Monument according to the design was $100,000.

The City Council accepted the design, and authorized the committee to contract for the erection of the Monument at an expense not exceeding the amount of the estimates. Work was immediately commenced on the foundation, and the committee advertised for proposals for building the Monument above the foundation. Upon opening these proposals it was found that the work could not be completed according to the design for less than $160,000. The committee reported the facts to the City Council; but failed to obtain an additional appropriation, and, upon the completion of the foundation, work was suspended.

Nothing further was done until 1870. In that year Aldermen Robert Cowdin and George O. Carpenter, and Councilmen Matthias Rich, William M. Flanders, and Joel Seaverns, were appointed a committee to consider and report upon the propriety of erecting a suitable Monument, and were authorized to procure designs for a Monument to be erected upon the foundation laid in 1866.

The committee advertised for designs for a Monument to cost not exceeding $75,000; and, in response to the request, designs were received from the following-named persons: —

1. Larkin G. Mead, sculptor, Florence.
2. John A. Jackson, sculptor, Florence.
3. Launt Thompson, sculptor, New York.
4. Peabody, Stearns & Chandler, architects, Boston.
5. C.-D. Lamb, Boston.
6. A. H. Lyon and C. J. Bateman, architects, Boston.
7. J. J. McNutt, Boston.
8. Faulkner, Clark & Dorr, architects, Boston.
9. L. Freres, Boston.
10. H. A. J.
11 and 12. Martin Milmore, sculptor, Boston.

13. R. W. Dalford, monumental architect, Boston.
14. E. G. Tucker, Boston.
15. G. Turini, sculptor, and W. W. Lummus, architect, Boston.
16. Richards & Park, architects, Boston.

Before making their report the committee placed the designs upon exhibition, for the purpose of getting an expression of opinion from citizens interested in the subject. In their report, made on the 31st of October, 1870, the committee say: —

Many citizens of cultivated taste availed themselves of the opportunity, and made a critical examination of the different designs. Taking into account the character of the competitors, and the high artistic merit which many of the designs possessed, there was remarkable unanimity in the selection of one, as specially adapted for the purpose and the location. This was extremely gratifying to the committee, because confirming their own unanimous choice. The design which they have accepted, and which they recommend for adoption by the City Council, was made by Mr. MARTIN MILMORE, a sculptor whose qualifications for such an important work are indisputable.

The committee recommended the passage of an order authorizing them to contract for the erection of a Monument on Flagstaff Hill, Boston Common, in accordance with a design made by Martin Milmore, at a cost not exceeding $75,000. This order was passed by the City Council, and approved by the Mayor, December 30, 1870.

In January, 1871, Aldermen Robert Cowdin, Samuel Talbot, Jr., and George W. Pope, and Councilmen Matthias Rich (President), William M. Flanders, Joseph H. Barnes, Isaac P. Gragg, and William C. Roberts, were appointed a joint special committee to have charge of the erection of the Soldiers' and Sailors' Monument, and under their direction a contract was concluded with Mr. Milmore, to erect the Monument complete above the foundation for the sum of $75,000.

LAYING THE CORNER-STONE.

On Monday, September 18, 1871, the corner-stone was laid, and the event was celebrated by an imposing public display. Business was generally suspended, the streets were thronged with people drawn together from all parts of the State to honor the occasion. Through all the streets marked for the route of the procession the decorations were numerous and beautiful. At two o'clock the procession moved in the following order : —

Chief of Police E. H. Savage, with Police Captains Vinal and Chase, and 24 mounted men.

Chief Marshal, General JOSEPH H. BARNES.

Chief of Staff, General R. H. Stevenson.
Adjutant-General, General Wm. H. Lawrence.
Aids: General Thomas Sherwin, General P. R. Guiney, Captain Isaac P. Gragg, Dr. Joel Seaverns.
Marshals: Colonel Thomas W. Clarke, Lowell B. Hiscock, Colonel Charles H. Hovey, Dr. Samuel A. Green, Captain Joseph S. Cary, Major George O. Carpenter, Colonel Charles B. Fox, Captain Barney Hull, Captain Wm. C. Roberts, Lieutenant G. A. Churchill.

FIRST BRIGADE, M.V.M.

Brigadier-General, Isaac S. Burrill, Boston.
Assistant Adjutant-General, rank, Lieutenant-Colonel, Hobart Moore, Boston.
Assistant Inspector-General, rank, Major, Solomon A. Bolster, Boston.

Assistant Quartermaster, rank, Captain, Thomas Decatur, W. Roxbury.
Engineer, rank, Captain, Brownell Granger, Boston.
Aid-de-camp, rank, Captain, Eben R. Frost, Boston.
Judge Advocate, Patrick A. Collins.
Gilmore's Band.
First Regiment of Infantry, Colonel George H. Johnson.
O'Connor's Band.
Ninth Regiment of Infantry, Colonel Bernard F. Finan.
Shawmut Band.
First Battalion of Infantry, Major Douglas Frazar.
Cleary's Band.
Second Battalion of Infantry, Major Louis Gaul.
First Battalion of Light Artillery, Major Charles W. Baxter.
Chelsea Band.
First Battalion of Cavalry, Lieutenant-Colonel, Albert Freeman.

DEPARTMENT OF MASSACHUSETTS — GRAND ARMY OF THE REPUBLIC.

General William Cogswell, Salem, Department Commander.

STAFF.

Henry B. Peirce, Assistant Adjutant-General.
W. S. Greenough, Assistant Quartermaster-General.
Charles O. Welch, Inspector.
Aids: Samuel Dalton, Charles H. Chase, William B. Sears, Edward J. Jones.

First Division, William Spaulding, Senior Vice-Dept.-Commander, commanding.
Aids: J. E. Ames, Walter Everett, H. R. Sibley, G. W. Daniels, G. H. W. Herrick.

FIRST BRIGADE.

Abner Coleman, Post 3, commanding.
National Band, Taunton.
Post 1, New Bedford, F. H. Forbes, commander.

Post 3, Taunton, A. Coleman, commander.
Post 6, Holliston, A. E. Chamberlain, commander.
Post 7, Boston, W. H. Cundy, commander.
Post 8, Middleboro', J. E. Cushman, commander.
Tremont Band.
Post 11, Charlestown, G. H. Long, commander.

SECOND BRIGADE.
George S. Worcester, Post 15, commanding.
Bond's Band.
Post 15, Boston, G. S. Worcester, commander.
Post 18, Ashland, G. C. Fiske, commander.
Post 21, Needham, J. E. Fiske, commander.
Post 23, East Boston, S. M. Weale, commander.
Post 26, Roxbury, Brownell Granger, commander.
Post 29, Waltham, H. S. Sherman, commander.

THIRD BRIGADE.
J. W. Smith, Post 30, commanding.
Suffolk Band.
Post 30, Cambridgeport, J. W. Smith, commander.
Post 32, South Boston, C. A. Cunningham, commander.
Post 33, Woburn, A. S. Leslie, commander.
Post 34, Salem, J. G. Bovey, commander.
Post 35, Chelsea, Henry Wilson, Jr., commander.
Post 40, North Weymouth, F. A. Bicknell, commander.

FOURTH BRIGADE.
J. P. Maxfield, Post 42, commanding.
Dunstable Band.
Post 42, Lowell, J. P. Maxfield, commander.
Post 43, Marlborough, C. F. Morse, commander.
Post 52, North Easton, G. H. Bates, commander.
Post 56, Cambridge, J. A. Munroe, commander.
Post 57, East Cambridge, G. H. Howard, commander.
Post 58, Weymouth, C. W. Hastings, commander.
Post 60, Whitinsville, R. R. Clark, commander.

THE ARMY AND NAVY MONUMENT. 19

Second Division, S. E. Chamberlain, Junior Vice-Dept.-Commander, commanding.

Rimbachs' Band.

FIRST BRIGADE.

A. St. John Chambré, Post 72, commanding.
Post 62, Newton, G. F. Brackett, commander.
Post 63, Natick, R. T. Nash, commander.
Post 64, Clinton, A. S. Davidson, commander.
Post 65, Warren, F. H. Moore, commander.

Mystic Band.

Post 66, Medford, John Hutchins, commander.
Post 68, Dorchester, J. T. Ward, Jr., commander.
Post 72, Stoughton, A. St. John Chambré, commander.

SECOND BRIGADE.

T. S. Atwood, Post 73, commanding.

American Band, Providence.

Post 73, Abington, T. S. Atwood, commander.
Post 74, East Abington, Lewis Reed, commander.
Post 76, Plymouth, C. B. Stoddard, commander
Post 86, Maynard, G. Babcock, commander.
Post 87, South Braintree, J. M. Stevens, commander.
Post 88, Quincy, W. G. Sheen, commander.

THIRD BRIGADE.

J. D. Billings, Post 94, commanding.

American Band, Boston.

Post 90, Danvers, W. W. Eaton, commander.
Post 94, Canton, J. D. Billings, commander.
Post 104, Hingham, P. N. Sprague, commander.
Post 105, West Medway, G. E. Pond, commander.
Post 110, Randolph, H. C. Alden, commander.
Post 113, Boston, C. G. Attwood, commander.

FOURTH BRIGADE.

G. M. Fiske, Post 117, commanding.

Carter's Band.

Post 117, Medfield, G. M. Fiske, commander.
Post 124, East Bridgewater, W. H. Osborne, commander.
Post 125, South Boston, W. W. Doherty, commander.
Post 134, Boston, G. C. Patterson, commander.
Post 139, Somerville, C. F. King, commander.
Post 142, South Framingham, C. H. Fuller, commander.
Post 143, Brookline, G. P. Richardson, commander.

Brown's Brigade Band.

Boston Independent Cadets, Lieut.-Col. F. W. Palfrey.
His Excellency Governor Claflin, Council and Staff, His Honor Mayor Gaston, Martin Milmore, Sculptor, and the Monument Committee, in carriages.

Grand Lodge of Massachusetts, F. & A. M., Charles Levi Woodbury, Grand Master, in carriages.

Germania Band.

Ancient and Honorable Artillery Company, Capt. Edwin C. Bailey; First Lieut., Capt. John Mack; Second Lieut., Capt. Richard M. Barker; Adj., Capt. Edwin R. Frost.

City Government of Boston, in carriages.

Boston Fire Department, under command of Chief Engineer John S. Damrell.

The route of the procession was through Charles, Beacon, Arlington, Boylston, Berkeley, and Tremont streets, Union Park, Washington street, Temple place, Tremont street, Scollay's square, Hanover, Blackstone, Clinton, Commercial, State, Washington, Summer, Chauncy, Essex, Boylston, and Tremont streets, to West-street entrance of the Common.

Arriving at the West-street gate, the military and grand army posts marched to the hill, and formed in mass to witness the ceremony of laying the corner-stone. The ceremony began with the overture to "Stradella," rendered by an orchestra of one hundred selected musicians, directed by M. Arbuckle. The Rev. Warren H. Cudworth then offered the following prayer: —

PRAYER BY REV. WARREN H. CUDWORTH.

Almighty Author of our being, accept the heartfelt thanks of Thy children, gathered in this place to-day, for the providential care which has watched over the trying vicissitudes of their recent struggle for continued existence as a free and united nation; and graciously bless the occasion which has called them together, that they may suitably commemorate the fortitude and fidelity, the patriotism and bravery of those heroic men, on land and water, who went from this city during the recent war for the preservation of the Union, and nobly laid upon their country's altar, time, strength, limb, health, and even life.

May we never forget the devotion to duty, the patient endurance, the entire self-sacrifice they exhibited throughout the war, and may the monumental shaft which shall rise above the corner-stone this day consecrated to their memory transmit to future generations the record of their unswerving loyalty to law, to the Union, and the Constitution. Comfort, we beseech Thee, the bereaved relatives and friends of those who will return no more, and bless their surviving comrades in arms gathered to participate with us in these solemn services.

Extend Thy favor, O God, to those who have been elevated to rule over us, whether in our cities, our States, or in the nation at large. May harmony increase, and good-will more and more prevail throughout our borders, and the peace now restored to our councils become the permanent and unchangeable condition of our national life and being.

Impart wisdom from on high to the City Authorities who shall regulate the proceedings of this occasion; to him who shall address us upon the lessons of the hour; to the organized associations of our fellow-citizens assembled here, and all others interested in this act of grateful and patriotic remembrance; and unto Thee, God over all, blessed forever, be glory, honor, and praise, world without end. Amen.

The Grand Army choir of one hundred voices then sang to the air of "Glory Hallelujah," the following hymn, written by Dexter Smith: —

I.

The bud that Spring-time nurtures with its showers and its sun,
Bursts into sweetest blossom ere the Summer days are done,
And Autumn brings fruition to the flow'r that Spring begun,
  As Time goes marching on !

CHORUS: — Glory, Glory, Hallelujah !
  Glory, Glory, Hallelujah !
  Glory, Glory, Hallelujah !
  As Time goes marching on !

II.

The bud of Liberty sprung forth upon old Bunker Hill,
It blossomed down at Mexico, with hues unfading still ;
Its beauties were reflected in each river and each rill,
  As Peace went marching on !

CHORUS: — Glory, Glory, Hallelujah, etc.

III.

When thro' the Spring-time of our land Rebellion's foul blast came,
The blooming Rose of Liberty set all the North aflame ;

Its red and white and blue combined to weave fair Freedom's name,
    As Peace went marching on!

CHORUS: — Glory, Glory, Hallelujah, etc.

IV.

Our brothers held the flow'r aloft as side by side they trod
The soil that welcomed hero-lives to graves beneath its sod,
And souls of sweetest fragrance there exhaled to Freedom's God,
    As Peace went marching on!

CHORUS: — Glory, Glory, Hallelujah, etc.

V.

Now Autumn flings her banners wide; her rainbow hues increase,
The harvest God has promised us on earth shall never cease;
The gory flow'r has ripened, and its shining fruit is Peace,
    The Peace that marches on!

CHORUS: — Glory, Glory, Hallelujah, etc.

VI.

God bless the harvest that is ours beneath the Union sky,
The seeds of freedom He has sown shall ever fructify,
Till "Peace on earth — good-will to man" their fruits shall multiply,
    As Peace goes marching on!

CHORUS: — Glory, Glory, Hallelujah, etc.

At the conclusion of the hymn Alderman Robert Cowdin, chairman of the committee, made the following address: —

Your Excellency, Your Honor, and Gentlemen of the City Government, — The Monument to be erected here is not to commemorate a fratricidal strife. It is not to stand as a memorial of the triumph of one section of the Union over another. The citizens of Boston would never have sanctioned its construction for such an object. It has a nobler purpose. The words of Webster at the dedication of the Bunker Hill Monument may be used here with increased emphasis: "This column stands on Union." It is to commemorate the heroic services and sacrifices of those who were instrumental in establishing upon an enduring foundation the Union of the States that we are gathered here to-day.

Of the part which the City Government and the citizens of Boston took in that mighty struggle for the preservation of the Union it is not for me to speak. My duty on this occasion is simply to state, in as few words as possible, what the committee entrusted with the erection of this Monument have done, and what they purpose doing. In 1866, the year following the close of the war, a committee of the City Council was appointed to consider the expediency of erecting a Monument in some prominent place in this city to commemorate the services of those of our citizens who fell in defence of the Union. The committee reported unanimously in favor of erecting a Monument, and recommended that plans and estimates should be procured. The recommendation was adopted, and, in November of that year, designs prepared by Hammatt Billings were submitted to the City Council. With great unanimity the government passed an order authorizing the committee to erect a Monument on this spot, at an expense not exceeding one hundred thousand dollars. After the foundation had been laid it appeared that the estimates upon which the committee had been authorized to proceed were too low, and that a considerable additional sum would be needed to carry out the design. The municipal year was then near its close, and the City Council refused to grant an additional appropriation without further consideration. Other matters claimed the attention of several succeeding governments, and it was not until last year that definite action was again taken on the subject. A committee was then appointed with authority to receive designs for a Monument to be erected on the foundation laid in 1866. In calling for designs the committee fixed the limit of expenses at seventy-five thousand dollars, and offered a premium of five hundred dollars to the successful competitor. Sixteen drawings, of various degrees of excellence, were submitted, and after careful consideration the choice of the committee fell unanimously upon a design presented by Martin Milmore. The City Council approved the selection, and the committee was authorized to contract for the construction of a Monument, in accordance with the design, for a sum not exceeding seventy-five thousand dollars. As the necessary specifications could not be prepared in season for the committee to execute their contract before their term of office expired, the subject was brought to the attention of the present City Government early in this year, and a new committee was appointed with full power to proceed with the work. The necessary plans and specifications having been prepared, the contract with Mr. Milmore was executed by the committee, acting in behalf of the city, on the second day of June last.

It thus appears that the proposition to erect a Monument in this city has received the favorable action of three different City Councils and the approval of three Mayors. I need not speak to citizens of Boston of Mr. Milmore's qualifications for carrying out his noble design. What he has already accomplished in the plastic art bears the stamp of genius.

The time for completing this work cannot of course be definitely fixed now. I can only say that there will be no unreasonable delay. The character of the work is such that it cannot be hurried to a conclusion without the liability of producing an unsatisfactory result.

On concluding, Alderman Cowdin called upon His Honor Mayor Gaston, who spoke as follows: —

ADDRESS OF THE MAYOR.

We meet to-day to engage in a service which is designed to honor the dead; but it is a service which will also ennoble the living. The fame of those who sleep needs not the aid of monumental stones. The story of their devotion will outlast any tablets on which it may be written. Their title to a hallowed remembrance is assured and secure; but the living must vindicate their character by paying just tribute to the memory of the honored dead; and they will come from the proper performance of that duty with hearts made better and with aspirations made higher by such a labor.

This service, so solemn, so pure, and so ennobling, brings us together now with united hands and hearts, and with accordant voices, to begin to raise and to dedicate to the memory of those who gave their lives to their country a Monument which shall, with its silent speech, give to the present and carry to the future a story of their sacrifice and glory.

Let us bring to this service the spirit which befits such

a labor. In this presence let us forget all diversities of faith and opinion, and unite with a common devotion in the solemn and yet grand duties of the hour.

Here the spirit of strife and dissension must stand rebuked. It must carry its dissonant voices elsewhere. This place and this hour have duties too sacred for its presence. Here and now we are thinking of those who, whatever might have been their differences of faith, " stood shoulder by shoulder on the perilous ridges of battle," and mingled in a common current their blood shed in the defence of their country. Here and now the memory of the heroic and brave men, many of whom are sleeping as they fought side by side, is rushing upon us and filling our hearts with sorrow, with pride, and with love. Let no spirit which is unworthy of fellowship with such emotions invade the solemn beauty and harmony of this occasion.

In the spring of 1861 the roar of arms was heard. It announced that rebellion had thrown off its disguise, and that civil war had begun. The issues of the struggle then were (as they were well described by another), " whether the work of our noble fathers of the Revolutionary and Constitutional age shall perish or endure ; whether the great experiment in national polity which binds a family of free republics in one united government — the most hopeful plan for combining the home-bred blessings of a small state with the stability and power of a great empire — shall be treacherously and shamefully stricken down in the moment of its most successful operation, or whether it shall be bravely, patriotically, triumphantly, maintained."

These issues were to be determined upon the field of

battle. Then from the North, from the East, and from the West, hosts of patriotic and devoted men came to the defence of the standard of their country.

> They came " as the winds come when forests are rended."
> They came " as the waves come when navies are stranded; "

and by their steadfast valor, shown on many a well-fought field, they rescued the nation from the hands of treason, and gave it back to liberty and to law.

To the living soldiers we recognize our deep and lasting obligation, and to the memories of the dead we render our tributes of love and veneration.

> " How sleep the brave, who sink to rest,
> By all their country's wishes blest!
> When spring, with dewy fingers cold,
> Returns to deck their hallowed mould,
> She there shall dress a sweeter sod
> Than Fancy's feet have ever trod.
>
> " By fairy hands their knell is rung;
> By forms unseen their dirge is sung;
> There Honor comes, a pilgrim gray,
> To bless the turf that wraps their clay;
> And Freedom shall awhile repair,
> To dwell, a weeping hermit, there."

The great struggle was, for a long time anterior to its inception, the subject of a despairing prophecy. But the prophets who foresaw it saw beyond it only disaster and ruin. No prophetic vision penetrated far enough beyond the veil which conceals the future from the present to see the nation rise from the struggle to a greater strength and to a grander life than before. No one saw far enough into the future to see her as she is to-day, "great, glorious, and free," advancing in her new career of prosperity and power to a higher destiny and to a more resplendent success. Would that the life of that great statesman and patriot who in his generation fought so valiantly against treason and disunion, the memory of whose eloquence still surrounds yonder shaft of revolutionary fame, might have been spared to this day, so that his "last lingering glance" might have beheld "the gorgeous ensign of the Republic known and honored throughout the earth," still more highly "advanced, its arms and trophies streaming in their original lustre, not a stripe erased or polluted, nor a single star obscured, and everywhere spread all over in characters of living light, blazing on its ample folds as they float over the sea and over the land, and in every true American heart,—Liberty and union, now and forever, one and inseparable."

It is my privilege, in behalf of the City of Boston to greet this great assemblage of people, and to invite them to join with us in laying the corner-stone of a structure which art is seeking to make worthy of those to whose honor it is to be reared. In the great and successful struggle for the preservation of our liberty, our constitution, and our Union, Boston proved herself to be true to her traditions and her history. Endangered liberty found in the place where "her infancy was rocked" worthy descendants and successors of those who were faithful to her in the days of her weakness.

Boston is proud of this new chapter in her history. The sons, nurtured in her ancient faith and inspired by her old patriotism, have carried to victory the same standard which their fathers left to them. Many of them have fallen while at the posts of duty on the sea and on the land — and to their memory she is this day beginning to rear a Monument almost within the reach of the shadow of that shaft to which nearly forty millions of people look with pride and veneration.

The names of many of the heroic men of this city who gave their lives to our defence now rush upon my recollection; but the time which this occasion allows to me will not permit me to render to them individually the tributes which are justly their due. They have passed from us in the pride of their strength and of their beauty.

> "The hand of the reaper
> Takes the ears that are hoary,
> But the voice of the weeper
> Wails manhood in glory.
> The autumn winds rushing
> Waft the leaves that are searest,
> But our flowers were in flushing
> When blighting was nearest."

Their deaths have made homes desolate, and yet glorious; hearts sorrowful, and yet proud.

They have gone to their rest; but they sleep in glory, and a grateful city is now, with its most imposing and august ceremonies, engaged in a solemn service to their honor.

Let the structure which we this day begin to rear proceed to its full completion. Let art give to it her choicest forms of beauty. Let it remain from age to age to illustrate the glory of the dead and the devotion of the living, and let it carry with it from generation to generation the same spirit of liberty to which it owes its origin.

His Honor's address was followed by the singing of the "Star-Spangled Banner" by the choir, after which Alderman Cowdin turned to the members of the Grand Lodge of Massachusetts, F. & A.M., and said: —

Most Worshipful Grand Master, — In behalf of the City Government I request you to lay the corner-stone of this Monument according to the usages of your ancient order, and to deposit under it this metallic box, containing an engraved plate and certain historical documents.

On being addressed by Alderman Cowdin, Acting Grand Master CHARLES LEVI WOODBURY arose and responded: —

From time immemorial it has been the custom of the Ancient and Honorable Fraternity of Free and Accepted Masons, when requested so to do, to lay, with ancient forms, the corner-stone of buildings erected for the worship of God, for charitable objects, for the purposes of the administration of justice and free government, and for the erection of such public monuments as, while appropriately of patriotic and common interests to the citizens of the Commonwealth to which we belong, may not vex Masonic harmony by the inroad of political feeling or discussion.

The corner-stone, therefore, we may lay in accordance with our law; and thus testifying our respect for the City of Boston, and our appreciation of the patriotic dead whose released spirits now hover near, we shall proceed in accordance with ancient usage. And as the first duty of Masons, in any undertaking, is to invoke the blessing of the Great Architect upon their work, we will now unite with our Grand Chaplain in an address to the Throne of Grace.

At the conclusion of the prayer, a sealed box containing the following articles was placed in a cavity prepared for it in the corner-stone: —

1. Inaugural Address of Mayor Gaston.
2. Report of Joint Special Committee on the Erection of an Army and Navy Monument.
3. The President's Message, 1870.
4. Finance Report, 1870.
5. Annual Report of the Chief of the Bureau of Statistics, 1870.
6. Auditor's Report, 1870–71.
7. Boston Municipal Register, 1871.
8. Twenty-first Semi-annual Report of the Superintendent of Public Schools.
9. Statistics of the Public Schools of Boston.
10. Topographical Description of Boston. (Shurtleff.)
11. Oration before the City Authorities of Boston, by Horace Binney Sargent, July 4, 1871.
12. Map of Boston, 1870.
13. Map of Dorchester, 1870.
14. Lithograph of Monument.
15. Copies of all the Daily Papers printed in Boston.
16. Copies of the Invitation of the City Council to attend the Ceremonies at laying the Corner-stone.
17. List of Members of the Grand Lodge of Freemasons of Masachusetts.
18. A Solid Silver Slab, with the following inscription: —

The Corner-Stone of a
MONUMENT
Erected by the City of Boston

In Honor of Her Patriotic Sons who Fell in

The Defence of the Union during the Rebellion of 1861-65,

And in Commemoration of the Heroic Sacrifices

Of All Classes of Her Citizens

During a Struggle which Confirmed the Integrity of

The Republic,

And Secured Universal Liberty throughout the Land.

Laid on the Eighteenth Day of September, A.D. 1871,

In Presence of

The City Government and Citizens of Boston,

By William Sewall Gardner,

Grand Master Grand Lodge of Freemasons, Massachusetts.

Committee on the Erection of the Monument.

Robert Cowdin, Samuel Talbot, Jr., George W. Pope, Matthias Rich, William M. Flanders, Joseph H. Barnes, Isaac P. Gragg, William C. Roberts.

Sculptor.

Martin Milmore.

City Government for 1871.

[Here follows a list of the Aldermen and Councilmen.]

The stone having been adjusted the Masonic ceremonial was performed by the Acting Grand Master, assisted by the following officers: —

Acting Deputy Grand Master, Charles R. Train.
Acting Senior Grand Warden, Sereno D. Nickerson.
Junior Grand Warden, Elijah W. Burr.
Acting Grand Treasurer, Newell A. Thompson.
Grand Chaplain, Alonzo H. Quint, D.D.
Grand Marshal, William T. Grammer.

At the conclusion of the Masonic ceremonies, "America" was sung by the choir and assembly, and the audience was then dismissed with a benediction by the Rev. Mr. Cudworth.

The exercises began at about half-past five o'clock and lasted until seven.

ARRANGEMENTS FOR THE DEDICATION.

In 1872 Mr. Milmore went to Rome, where he spent the ensuing five years in modelling his designs. The contract provided that the statues, as well as the body of the Monument, should be of granite, and the bas-reliefs of white marble. Mr. Milmore, however, became convinced that the proper execution of the work required a change in the materials, and he therefore wrote to the committee having the matter in charge, asking to be allowed to substitute bronze for granite and marble in the statues and bas-reliefs, and offering to assume the additional expense which the change involved. The committee, after consulting with competent art critics, assented to the proposed change.

In January, 1877, Aldermen Francis Thompson and Charles W. Wilder, and Councilmen Lowell B. Hiscock, James J. Flynn, and James H. Nugent, were appointed to have charge of the erection of the Army and Navy Monument.

Mr. Milmore arrived home in April, 1877, and informed the committee that he would deliver the Monument to the city on the 17th of September. The committee immediately communicated the intelligence to the City Council, in the following report: —

The Joint Special Committee, appointed to take charge of the erection of the Army and Navy Monument on Boston Common, beg leave to report that they are in receipt of a communication from Martin Milmore, announcing that the Monument will be completed and ready for dedication on the 17th of September next. The committee hasten to convey this gratifying intelligence to the City Council, believing that the completion of this Monument to the memory of our heroic dead will be an event in the history of this city which it will doubtless be desired to commemorate in a befitting manner. It will be no ordinary occasion. On that day the City of Boston will discharge a debt long due her sons who maintained her renown in the great struggle for the maintenance of republican institutions. She will dedicate a memorial which will hand down to posterity in enduring bronze and granite the record of their virtues, which will serve to stimulate the patriotism and quicken the loyalty of all coming generations. Our citizens expect that the dedication of this Monument will be made the occasion for a demonstration which will do honor to our municipality. The gratitude of the people to those who, obedient to the call of duty and patriotism, went forth from our midst to battle in the cause of liberty and right, has never grown cold, and the completion of a testimonial of a grateful people to the prowess and self-devotion of those who died in the defence of our imperilled nationality should be commemorated in a manner alike creditable to ourselves and honorable to the memory of our departed heroes. The committee recommend that the 17th day of September next be selected as the day for the dedication of the Monument. It will be the two hundred and forty-seventh anniversary of the settlement of Boston, and it appears peculiarly fitting that it should be selected as the day upon which to dedicate a public work of such historical interest as the Army and Navy Monument. Believing that the importance of the occasion requires that the preparation for its observance should be commenced at an early day, your committee respectfully ask the City Council for instructions as to what arrangements shall be made for dedicating the Monument.

The City Council accepted the report, and passed an order authorizing the committee to make the necessary arrangements for dedicating the Monument on the 17th of September, at a cost not exceeding twenty-two thousand five hundred dollars.

The committee, believing that one of the most interesting features of the occasion would be a procession in which the veterans of the war should bear a prominent part, conferred with the representatives of the various military and civic organizations in the city, and received assurances of the hearty coöperation of the several bodies. Col. Augustus P. Martin was accordingly appointed to act as Chief Marshal of the procession.

It was decided to hold the dedicatory exercises on a platform to be erected at the base of the Monument; to invite the M.W. Grand Lodge of F. and A. Masons of Massachusetts to perform the dedicatory service peculiar to that order; to invite the Hon. Charles Devens to deliver an oration, and the Rev. Warren H. Cudworth to act as Chaplain of the day; to decorate the City Hall; to illuminate the Monument, and to provide an evening concert on the Common. Commodore Foxhall A. Parker, Commandant of the Navy Yard, besides tendering to the City Government an escort, consisting of the marines and sailors attached to the station, volunteered to fire a salute at morning, noon, and night.

The Chief Marshal, in a circular issued on the 11th of September, made the following announcement in regard to the procession: —

The United States Marine Corps, Col. Jones commanding, is to report to Hon. Francis Thompson, Chairman, at City Hall, at 9.30 o'clock, A.M.

The First Corps of Cadets is to form at 10.30 o'clock, A.M., on Charles-street mall, right resting at Boylston street, left extending toward Beacon street, and is to escort His Excellency the Governor, with his staff, thence to his position in the column.

The militia, as it passes the State House, will be reviewed by His Excellency the Governor.

The Second Corps of Cadets, acting as special escort to the Chief

Marshal. will form at 10.30 A.M., on Boylston-street mall, right resting opposite Carver street.

The First Brigade, M.V.M., is to form on Essex and Kingston streets, the right resting at corner of Essex and Washington streets.

The Second Brigade, M.V.M., is to form on Charles street, right resting at the corner of Boylston street.

The First Division, consisting of the Department of Massachusetts, Grand Army of the Republic, will form on the east sidewalk of Tremont street, right resting at Boylston street, left extending south toward Chester square.

The Second Division, consisting of veteran organizations, will form on the west sidewalk of Tremont street, right resting at Berkeley street, left extending north toward Boylston street.

The Third Division will form on Castle street, right resting at the corner of Tremont street, left extending toward Washington street.

The Fourth Division will form on Berkeley street, right resting at Tremont, left prolonged toward Boylston street.

The Fifth Division will form in Berkeley street, right resting at Commonwealth avenue, left prolonged to the west on Beacon street.

The Sixth Division will form in Marlborough street, right resting at Berkeley street, left prolonged toward Exeter.

The Seventh Division will form in two subdivisions, the first consisting of the Irish Charitable Societies, and the Ancient Order of Hibernians, under the command of Timothy Deasey, Marshal, on Commonwealth avenue; the second, consisting of the Catholic Total Abstinence Union and the St. James Total Abstinence Society, under command of Mr. Patrick H. Barry, Marshal, on Newbury street; the right of each subdivision resting on Berkeley street, the left prolonged toward Gloucester street.

The Chief Marshal recommends that the march of the First and Second Divisions be made, so far as practicable, in column of companies or platoons.

The barges for the conveyance of the disabled veterans, other than members of the Grand Army, will stand in Chandler, near Tremont street. Barges for the Grand Army will be placed at such points as the Chief of the First Division may designate.

Head-quarters of the Chief Marshal will be at Park square, in front of the Providence Railroad station. The General Staff will report to him there at 9 o'clock.

Chiefs of Divisions will establish their head-quarters at the points indicated above as the right of their respective divisions.

Officers of the Army, Navy, and Marine corps of the United States, and ex-officers of the volunteer service, not on special duty for the occasion, are requested to appear in the uniform of their rank.

General, Field and Staff officers marching with the veteran division, and officers commanding veteran organizations, are requested to appear mounted.

Soldiers and sailors not connected with any organization in column will report to Col. E. O. Shepard, commanding Second Division.

All army, corps, and veteran society badges are to be worn.

The formation of the column will be completed at 10.30 o'clock, and at 11 o'clock a gun will be fired and the procession will move over the following route: Tremont street, Chester square, Shawmut avenue, Roxbury street, Guild Row, Dudley, Warren, Washington, Summer, High, Congress, Milk, Broad, State, Devonshire, New Washington, Hanover, Court, Washington, School, Beacon, and Charles streets to the Common.

Citizens are requested to decorate their stores and residences situated along the line of march.

A line of telegraph has been established over the entire route, with stations at the following points: Park square, corner Tremont and Dover streets; Chester square and Shawmut avenue; Dudley street, opposite Highland Railroad depot; Metropolitan Railroad station, Washington street; Washington street and Blackstone square; Washington and Asylum streets; Washington and Summer streets; Post-office square; State, near Devonshire street; Hanover and Court streets; City Hall; and corner of Beacon and Charles streets. At these stations placards will from time to time be exhibited, showing the position of the head of the column.

Any organization reaching the ground after the departure of the division to which it was assigned, will report to the Chief of the next succeeding one not already in motion.

Through the courtesy of Commodore Foxhall A. Parker, Commandant

United States Navy Yard, a salute will be fired at the Navy Yard, Charlestown, morning, noon, and sunset.

The Committee on the Monument announce that the Monument will be illuminated during the evening.

Chiefs of Divisions are requested to transmit to these head-quarters, on the day following the march, consolidated reports of their commands.

By order of
A. P. MARTIN,
Chief Marshal.

THOMAS SHERWIN,
Adjutant-General.

DESCRIPTION OF THE MONUMENT.

GENERAL DESCRIPTION OF THE MONUMENT.

The Monument erected by the City of Boston in memory of her sons who fell in the war of the Rebellion stands upon Flagstaff Hill, the highest point of unoccupied ground within the limits of the city proper. Rising proudly from this elevation to a height of more than seventy feet, its graceful column of granite forms a special point of attraction for the thousands who pass it in the daily ebb and flow of business and pleasure, and serves as a perpetual reminder of the martyrs whose death it commemorates, and the sacredness of the cause for which they perished.

The shaft is of white Maine granite, quarried by the Hallowell Granite Company, which executed the work after the plans furnished by Mr. Martin Milmore. The foundation upon which it rests is of solid masonry, cruciform in shape, built up from a depth of sixteen feet to the ground level.

The first course of the structure consists of a platform, irregular in form, covering an area thirty-eight feet square. It is reached by three steps, each having a rise of fifteen inches, with a tread of two feet. From this platform rises a plinth nine feet in height with projecting pedestals at each of the four corners, giving this portion of the Monument the exact shape of a square fort with bastions. These pedestals are embellished upon the sides with single, and in front with double, wreaths of laurel, elaborately cut in *alto-rilievo*. Upon them stand the four bronze figures, each eight feet in height, representing Peace, History, the Army and Navy. On the four sides of the plinth between the pedestals are bronze *mezzo-rilievos*, five feet six inches in length by two feet six inches in width, symbolical of incidents of the war. The relief that meets the eye of the spectator in front represents the departure of a regiment for the field; another symbolizes a naval engagement; the third has for its subject the labors of the Sanitary Commission; and the fourth shows the return of the regiments at the close of the conflict.

Upon the plinth rests the pedestal proper, fourteen feet three inches in height, terminating in a cornice, or surbase. The four sides of the die are panelled. In that facing the South is cut in bold letters, illuminated with gold leaf, the following inscription, furnished by President Charles W. Eliot, of Harvard College: —

> TO THE MEN OF BOSTON
> WHO DIED FOR THEIR COUNTRY
> ON LAND AND SEA IN THE WAR
> WHICH KEPT THE UNION WHOLE
> DESTROYED SLAVERY
> AND MAINTAINED THE CONSTITUTION
> THE GRATEFUL CITY
> HAS BUILT THIS MONUMENT
> THAT THEIR EXAMPLE MAY SPEAK
> TO COMING GENERATIONS

From the surbase of the pedestal rises the column, which is of the Roman-Doric order, and ornate in character. Its effectiveness is largely enhanced by the figures in *alto-rilievo* grouped

about its base, representing the four sections of the Union, — North, South, East, and West. They are eight feet in height, and, as is customary in the representation of allegorical figures, they are robed in classic drapery, which is skilfully and gracefully disposed.

The lower section of the shaft rises eight feet and six inches, ending with the first band, a beautifully sculptured wreath. Above this is the second section, or fluted part of the column, seven feet in height. Two plain sections of the shaft follow, the first six feet five inches, and the second six feet ten inches in height, separated by wreath-bands, terminating with a band bearing the emblematic stars, and surmounted by a capital, of graceful and striking design, seven feet square and elaborately carved. Above each side is sculptured an eagle with outspread wings in white marble.

The capstone, a circular block of granite, is two feet eleven inches thick, and five feet in diameter. Upon this stands the bronze statue of the Genius of America, the crowning glory of the Monument, — a structure which may justly be regarded as the finest example of memorial architecture erected in this country since the war.

Sealed boxes, containing papers and documents were placed beneath the base of the column by the City of Boston, the Grand Army of the Republic, and the Loyal Legion.

That deposited by the City of Boston contained the following articles : —

1. Copy of the Boston Municipal Register for 1877.
2. Acts and Resolves of Massachusetts passed in the year 1877.
3. Manual of the General Court of Massachusetts for 1877.
4. City Documents, Numbers 52, 103, 118, 132, of the year 1866.
5. City Document Number 98, of the year 1870.
6. A copy of the invitation sent to distinguished persons to attend the Dedicatory Ceremonies.

7. A copy of each of the Boston daily papers of July 28th.
8. A Plate with this inscription: —

THE ARMY AND NAVY MONUMENT WAS DEDICATED ON THE SEVENTEENTH
DAY OF SEPTEMBER, A.D. 1877.

RUTHERFORD B. HAYES, President of the United States.
ALEXANDER H. RICE, Governor of Massachusetts.
FREDERICK O. PRINCE, Mayor of Boston.

Committee of Arrangements.
FRANCIS THOMPSON, Chairman.
CHARLES W. WILDER.
LOWELL B. HISCOCK.
JAMES J. FLYNN.
JAMES H. NUGENT.

MARTIN MILMORE, Sculptor.
AUGUSTUS P. MARTIN, Chief Marshal.
JOSEPH MILMORE, Supervising Architect.

That deposited by the Grand Army of the Republic, Department of Massachusetts, contained the following memorial, with the list of articles annexed: —

THE GRAND ARMY OF THE REPUBLIC

Is a Fraternal, Loyal, and Charitable Association of honorably discharged soldiers and sailors, who aided in resisting the attempt of the slave-holding States of the American Union to secede from that Union of the United States of North America, in the great rebellion of the years 1861–1865; which rebellion, causing a gigantic civil war, then resulted in the emancipation of four millions of slaves, the supremacy of the Federal Government, and the consequent restoration of the Union.

The motto of this Association is "Fraternity, Charity, and Loyalty;" and the Association is divided into departments, coinciding territorially with States of the Union; and subdivided into smaller local organizations called Posts, devoted to the charitable care of soldiers and their families, widows, and orphans.

The Department of Massachusetts deposits in this box, under the Army and Navy Monument, erected by the City of Boston, the following articles, Anno Domini 1877: —

Duplicate of Post Charter.
Proceedings of National Encampments, 1866 to 1877, inclusive.
Rules and Regulations.
Service Book and Memorial Service.
One each of every kind of blank used in the G.A.R.
Roster of Department and complete file of General Orders, series of 1877.
A G.A.R. Badge: No. 2,521.
Alphabetical list of the battles of the War of the Rebellion.
Copy of the U. S. Army and Navy Pension Laws.

HORACE BINNEY SARGENT,
Department Commander.

JAMES F. MEECH,
Assistant Adjutant-General.

The following declaration and list of articles were deposited in the Monument by the Order of the Loyal Legion: —

The Commandery of the State of Massachusetts of the Military Order of the Loyal Legion of the United States deposits in the box to be placed under the Soldiers' and Sailors' Monument on Boston Common, September, A.D. 1877, the following documents, viz.: —

1. Charter and Organization of the Commandery of the State of Massachusetts of the Military Order of the Loyal Legion of the United States, March 4th and 6th, A.D. eighteen hundred and sixty-eight.
2. Constitution and By-Laws of the Order as adopted, April 9, 1865.
3. Diploma No. 534, and Ribbon of the Order.
4. Constitution and By-Laws of the Order, as amended by the Congress of the Order at New York, A.D. 1873.
5. Constitution and By-Laws of the Order, as amended by the Congress of the Order at Boston, Mass., April 11, 1877.
6. Annual Register of the Commandery of the State of Massachusetts for 1869.

7. Annual Register of the Commandery of the State of Massachusetts for 1870.

8. First Biennial Register of the Massachusetts Commandery for 1872 and 1873.

9. Second Biennial Register of the Massachusetts Commandery for 1874 and 1875.

10. Third Biennial Register of the Massachusetts Commandery for 1876 and 1877.

11. Officers of the Commandery of the State of Massachusetts for 1877 and 1878, elected May 2, 1877.

12. Names of the Committee of Arrangements of the Massachusetts Commandery of the M.O.L.L.U.S. for September 17, 1877.

13. Quadrennial Register of the New York Commandery for 1877.

14. Circulars of the Pennsylvania Commandery from August, 1865, to April, 1877.

15. Oration delivered by General Charles Devens, Commander of the Commandery, at Charlestown, Mass., June 17, 1875, in commemoration of the Centennial Anniversary of the Battle of Bunker Hill.

16. The Bill of Fare of a complimentary breakfast given by the Massachusetts Commandery at the Parker House, April 11, 1877, to representatives of the Congress of the Order.

17. The Bill of Fare of a complimentary dinner, given to the representatives of the Congress of the Order of the Commandery of the State of Massachusetts, at the Parker House, April 11, 1877.

18. Copies of the "Boston Evening Transcript" of June 16 and 19, 1875, containing a full report of the proceedings and exercises of the Centennial Anniversary of the Battle of Bunker Hill, including the banquet given by the Massachusetts Commandery of the M.O.L.L. U.S.

19. Copies of the "Boston Journal" of June 26 and 27, 1877, containing an authentic account of the visit to Boston of Rutherford B. Hayes, President of the United States, attended by his Cabinet, and of the reception and entertainment given to them and other distinguished guests by the Massachusetts Commandery of the M.O.L.L.U.S., at Young's Hotel, with Bill of Fare, on the evening of June 26, 1877.

20. Brochure of "Bunker Hill," an account of the Centennial, and

Heliotype views, compiled by George A. Coolidge, and presented by him.

INSCRIPTION ON THE BOX.

Deposited by the Commandery of the State of Massachusetts of the Military Order of the Loyal Legion of the United States, September, A.D. 1877, in the one hundred and second year of the Independence of the United States of America, and of the Order, the thirteenth.

By order of

BREVET-MAJOR-GENERAL CHARLES DEVENS,
Commander.

Attest: JAMES B. BELL, *Recorder.*
Official: JAMES B. BELL, *Recorder.*

AMERICA.

The ideal statue of America which crowns the Monument is a magnificent triumph of the sculptor's art. It was cast at the Woods' foundry, in Philadelphia, and is eleven feet in height, the banner reaching a further height of six feet. It represents a woman, majestically proportioned, clad in a flowing robe, which reaches, but does not cover, her sandalled feet. Over the robe is a loose tunic, bound in with a girdle at the waist, while a heavy mantle, clasped at the throat, is thrown back over the shoulders and falls the full length of her figure behind. Upon the head is a crown with thirteen stars.

The pose is wonderfully fine. The weight of the body rests upon the right foot, the left being slightly advanced. In the right hand, which rests upon the hilt of an unsheathed sword, are two wreaths of laurel, — one for those who perished in defence of the nation upon the sea, and the other for those who died for it upon the field of battle. The left hand grasps the broad banner of the Republic. The crowned head is slightly bowed, and the eyes cast down.

There is nothing of haughtiness nor defiance in attitude or expression. The figure does not symbolize America the conqueror, proud in her strength and defiant of her foes; but rather America the mourner, paying proud tribute to her loyal dead, whose bones lie upon every battle-field of the great South, toward which her face is turned.

PEACE.

At the right of the inscription upon the panel, and holding the most important place of the four bronzes grouped about the base of the die on which the column rests, is the statue of Peace. It represents a graceful female figure, robed in classic drapery, and seated upon a stone. Her right arm is raised and extended, and in her hand she holds an olive-branch; the left hand, resting upon the rock at her side, forms a support for her half-rising posture. The face is beautiful without being weak, and its expression is dignified and noble. Placed appropriately, with her face looking toward that section of the country from which she was banished so long, she seems to plead for common forgetfulness of the past, and promise a glorious and prosperous future.

THE SAILOR.

On the left of the Monument, looking toward the sea, is the statue which stands as the symbol of the United States Navy,— a sailor, in appropriate costume, standing in an easy attitude, the right hand resting upon a drawn cutlass, whose point touches the ground, the left hand supported by the hip. The graceful garb of the service affords the sculptor opportunity for a rare display of skill in the management of accessories. The open collar and knotted handkerchief, the navy cap, and other details of the dress and figure are given with wonderful truth and exactness. The whole figure is characterized by a boldness and freedom which one instinctively associates with the brave fellows who fought under Farragut, Porter, and Goldsborough, on the Mississippi and along the coast during the war.

Although the men of the navy had fewer opportunities to exhibit their personal valor in hand-to-hand conflicts during the four years' struggle than those of the army, they made no doubtful record when those opportunities did occur. The figure which Mr. Milmore's art has given us is expressive in a remarkable degree of personal courage and daring, and may be accepted as the ideal of the true American sailor.

HISTORY.

The figure representing the Muse of History is classic in its conception, and one of the finest of Mr. Milmore's creations. Like the statue of Peace, it occupies a sitting position, and is clad in simple Greek costume, whose artistically disposed folds reveal the superbly modelled form. The limbs are crossed. The left hand holds a tablet, which rests upon the knee; in the right is a stylus. The face is turned slightly away and upward, as if seeking for inspiration to properly record the deeds of the Grand Army now encamped upon the other shore. A wreath of laurel encircles the head, and a mantle, resting upon the left shoulder and falling below the waist, is drawn loosely across the knees, its broad, lateral folds breaking up the vertical lines of the drapery beneath.

There is a peculiar vigor about the design which makes it specially attractive. It combines the elements of grace and beauty in sculpture in a remarkable degree, and is striking without being obtrusively dramatic. The idea which is intended to be conveyed — the preservation of the names and memory of the deeds of the fallen, by historical record — is vividly presented.

THE SOLDIER.

The Army is represented by the figure of a soldier, standing at ease, with overcoat, belt, and accoutrements. His musket rests upon the ground. One hand lightly clasps its barrel; the other rests upon the muzzle. The pose is easy and graceful, and the countenance full of patriotic fire. The modelling of the various portions of the figure is skilfully done, and the difficulties attendant upon the treatment of the modern army costume so as to secure satisfactory results are successfully overcome. By many critics the statue is considered the finest of the group. It is, at any rate, characteristic of the typical American soldier.

In the carrying out of his idea the artist makes us feel that underneath the military garb there is the citizen, and not the hired fighter of a nation's battles; that the hands which hold the musket have done service in the arts of peace, and that, while the figure represents the armed defender of the people's rights, it also represents the people themselves.

DEPARTURE FOR THE WAR.

The bronze relief placed in the front of the Monument represents the departure of troops for the war, and introduces the portraits of several well-known citizens and eminent military men. In the background is the State House, past which the regiments are marching after having received their flags from the hands of the Governor. Near the head of the column rides Gen. B. F. Butler, and at his side Quartermaster-General John H. Reed. Further to the rear is seen Col. Thomas Cass, of the Ninth Regiment; behind him are Cols. Robert G. Shaw and Charles Russell Lowell, both of whom fell in the war.

In the centre of the group upon the State-House steps is Gov. Andrew. At his right stands Archbishop Williams, side

by side with the Rev. Alexander H. Vinton, D.D. Beyond the two are Turner Sargent and the Rev. Phillips Brooks. At the left of the Governor, leaning upon his cane, is Mr. C. O. Whitmore. Behind him stands Wendell Phillips, and near him, Henry W. Longfellow and Mr. P. B. Cheney.

The affecting incidents attendant upon the departure of troops for the field are depicted with sympathetic feeling, — the weeping wife with her infant in her arms; the father watching his son in the ranks with tearful yet proud eyes; the maiden bidding her betrothed farewell, — all these scenes, once so common, are perpetuated in the tablet. The whole number of figures is forty, although the grouping gives an idea of many more.

THE SANITARY COMMISSION.

The bronze relief which symbolizes the works of the Sanitary Commission during the war contains twenty-three figures, the most of them portraits. One of the two groups of which it is composed represents the prominent members of the Commission from this city in consultation; the other, the work in the field.

In the right-hand group the Hon. Alexander H. Rice is represented standing by a table, around which are piled boxes and packages marked "U.S.S.C." At his right stands E. R. Mudge, and at his left, the Rev. Dr. Gannett. In the background is seen the face of James Russell Lowell. Farther to the left of the table are George Ticknor, Col. W. W. Clapp, and the Hon. Marshal P. Wilder. There are several ladies in the group, variously engaged in the work connected with the preparation of the supplies to be forwarded to the field.

The left-hand group has for its background an ambulance, from which a wounded soldier has just been lifted by two of his companions. Of the two nurses in attendance, one supports the head of the wounded man, while the other, upon her knees, is busily engaged in preparing bandages.

Another soldier, who has been brought off the field, reclines half-fainting on the ground, with closed eyes, while a Sister of Mercy binds up his wounds. By his side stand the Rev. Edward Everett Hale, and Mrs. Parsons, a lady member of the Commission.

RETURN FROM THE WAR.

The most elaborate of the four reliefs is the "Return from the War," which contains forty figures. Peace has dawned upon the land, and after three years of fighting and marching, those of the battle-scarred veterans who have escaped death by bayonet and bullet have returned, and are here represented as having come to deliver up their tattered banners to the keeping of the State.

On the left of the relief a regiment is drawn up in front of the State House, and on the steps, where three years before he gave into its keeping the flag of the Commonwealth, the "great war governor," John A. Andrew, stands again to receive it. The ranks are broken by the mothers, wives, and children of the returning heroes, and all discipline is forgotten in the joy of meeting. The two figures on horseback, in advance, will be readily recognized as Generals Banks and Devens, and those in the rear as Generals Bartlett and Underwood.

Upon the steps to the left a group of ladies welcome the veterans home and bestow upon them wreaths of laurel. To the right of this group stands Dr. Edward Reynolds; then come in regular order of succession, Henry Wilson, Ex-Governor Claflin, Mayor Shurtleff, Judge Putnam, Charles Sumner, Charles W. Slack, James Redpath, and Joshua B. Smith. The group of soldiers on the right, with the flags of the regiment, serves admirably to balance the picture and give it true artistic value.

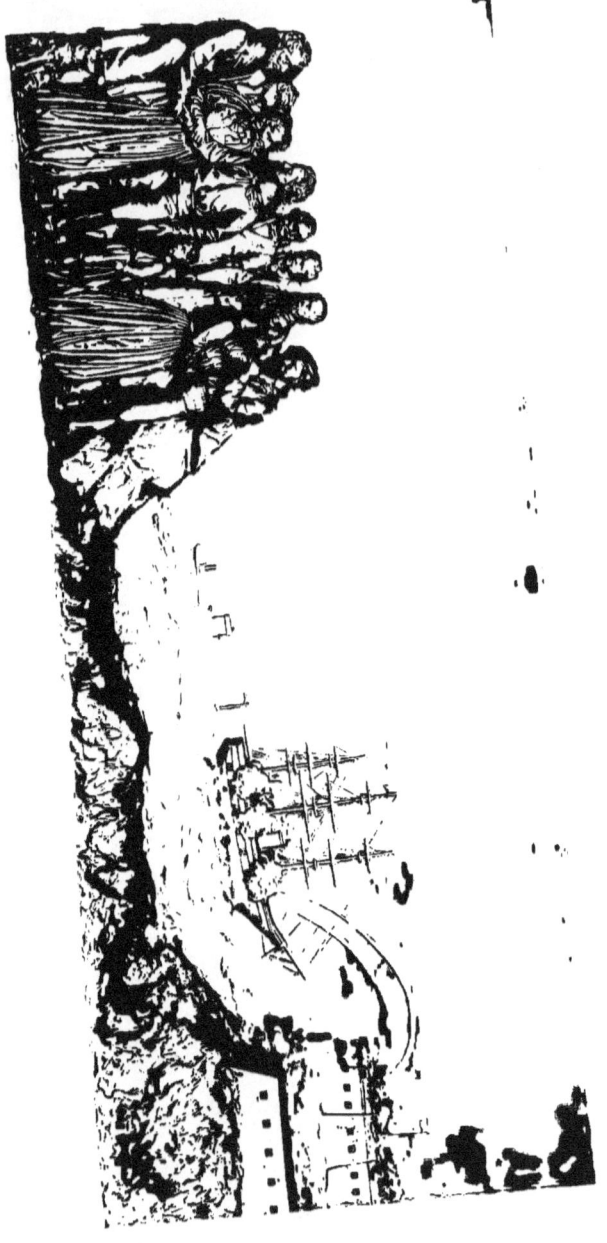

THE NAVY.

The fourth of the series of reliefs inserted in the four faces of the plinth commemorates the achievements of the Navy. It is properly divisible into two parts. The left-hand portion shows a group of eleven figures, and represents the departure of sailors from home at the call of the country. The central figure is that of a manly young sailor, who is taking leave of his family before joining his ship; with right hand extended he bids his father farewell; his mother clings to his arm, not in an appealing manner, but with a look of patriotic pride; a little child, too young to understand the necessity that takes his father from him, presses to his side, while the weeping wife covers her face with her hands and turns away. In another portion of the group a mother holds an infant up for its father to kiss.

The right of the design presents a view of a naval engagement. A low, rocky shore runs across the foreground, with the open sea beyond. In the right middle distance is a heavily constructed fort of masonry, and beyond, in the distance, is a second fort, standing upon a bluff. The centre is occupied by a monitor and a man-of-war, engaged in bombarding the more distant work, which vigorously resists the attack. No attempt is made by the artist to localize the fight; the design is simply emblematical of the many conflicts of the kind which took place during the war.

These four bronzes were cast by the Ames Company, Chicopee.

THE PROCESSION.

THE PROCESSION.

To the general public, the procession was probably the most interesting part of the ceremonies attending the dedication of the Monument. It was understood that it would be the last occasion upon which the survivors of the war would be gathered in such numbers in this city, and, while the uniforms of the militia and the regalias and banners of the societies added to the attractiveness of the procession, and as interesting features were much enjoyed by the spectators, the hearty enthusiasm with which the veteran soldiers were greeted proved how constantly and faithfully their services had been remembered.

Business was generally suspended throughout the city. Many buildings upon the route of the procession were handsomely decorated. The streets were thronged by an orderly, interested, and enthusiastic concourse of people.

The weather was threatening in the morning, but grew clear and hot before noon, while in the afternoon a slight shower, not sufficient to cause discomfort, freshened the air to a grateful degree.

At nine o'clock in the morning the members of the City Government, the guests of the city, and the persons invited to join the procession, assembled at the City Hall, and, escorted by the U. S. Marine Corps and Sailors, proceeded thence to their place in the procession.

The procession moved promptly at the hour assigned. The formation was as follows : —

THE ESCORT.

Detachment of Mounted Police under Chief of Police E. H. Savage, with Captains Chase and Graves as Aids.
Germania Band.
Second Corps of Cadets, Salem, escort to Chief Marshal.
Lieutenant-Colonel Samuel Dalton commanding,
Escorting

CHIEF MARSHAL AND STAFF.

Augustus P. Martin, Chief Marshal.

STAFF.

General Cornelius G. Attwood, Chief of Staff.
General Thomas Sherwin, Adjutant-General.
Major James B. Bell, Assistant Adjutant-General.
Colonel Edward G. Stevens, Assistant Adjutant-General.
Colonel Arnold A. Rand, Assistant Adjutant-General.
Colonel Joseph A. Ingalls, Chief Quartermaster.
Colonel Augustus N. Sampson, Assistant Quartermaster.
Lieutenant-Commander H. McMurtrie, Engineer.
Major John P. Ordway, Surgeon.
Lieutenant Edward B. Richardson, Chief Signal Officer.

AIDS TO THE CHIEF MARSHAL.

Maj. David T. Bunker,	Maj. George F. McKay,
Maj. John Bigelow,	Mr. S. B. Newton,
Col. Wm. L. Candler,	Lieut. W. M. Paul,
Gen. S. E. Chamberlain,	Mr. W. Prentiss Parker,
Maj. George T. Childs,	Mr. Gordon Prince,
Mr. Charles M. Clapp,	Col. James H. Rice,
Capt. John N. Coffin,	Mr. E. Roberts,
Lieut. W. A. Couthouy,	Mr. George C. Russell,
Capt. H. B. Clapp,	Mr. Arthur G. Richardson,
Col. J. W. Coveney,	Col. H. A. Stevens,
Col. George B. Dyer,	Lieut. T. A. Swords,
Mr. Henry L. Daggett, Jr.	Lieut. Henry Sherwin,

Col. E. R. Fowler,
Mr. Lyman B. Greenleaf,
Lieut. W. W. Humphrey,
Col. Charles H. Hovey,
Capt. A. W. Hersey,
Lieut. Charles S. Halliday,
Mr. Henry L. Hiscock,
Mr. Weston F. Hutchins,
Col. Edward J. Jones,
Capt. Geo. R. Kelso,
Maj. John E. Killian,
Mr. Edward W. Kinsley,
Maj. Everett Lane,
Col. William H. Long,
Lieut. H. W. Lyon,
Capt. R. S. Milton,
Capt. Charles L. Mitchell,
Maj. John W. Mahan,
Maj. B. F. Meservey,
Maj. L. W. Muzzey,

Capt. Dennis Meehan,
Col. John L. Stevenson,
Col. William W. Swan,
Gen. L. Stephenson, Jr.,
Lieut. Silas Sanborn,
Lieut.-Com. P. J. Stone, Jr.,
Col. James Tucker,
Maj. B. F. Talbot,
Capt. Benj. H. Ticknor,
Col. Louis N. Tucker,
Lieut. Henry A. Turner,
Mr. Newell A. Thompson,
Col. Henry Walker,
Mr. Charles W. Wilder, Jr.,
Col. Thomas Weston,
Maj. Charles B. Whittemore,
Mr. Francis H. Willcutt,
Lieut. H. E. Warner,
Lieut. E. B. Warren.

Cadet Band.

First Corps of Cadets, Boston, Lieut.-Col. Thomas F. Edmands commanding,

Escorting His Excellency ALEXANDER H. RICE, of Boston, Governor and Commander-in-Chief.

Major-Gen. James A. Cunningham, of Boston, Adjutant-General.
Col. Isaac F. Kingsbury, of Newton, Assistant Adjutant-General.
Col. C. Frank Luther, of Adams, Assistant Adjutant-General.
Col. John H. Rice, of Boston, Assistant Adjutant-General.
Lieut.-Col. Frederick Mason, of Taunton, Assistant Inspector-General.
Lieut.-Col. A. Hun Berry, of Lynn, Assistant Inspector-General.
Brig.-Gen. Wilmon W. Blackmar, of Boston, Judge Advocate-General.
Col. Henry G. Parker, of Boston, Assistant Quartermaster-General.
Brig.-Gen. William J. Dale, of North Andover, Surgeon-General.
Col. Joshua B. Treadwell, of Boston, Assistant Surgeon-General.

Col. William V. Hutchins, of Boston, Col. William A. Tower, of Lexington, Col. Arthur T. Lyman, of Boston, Col. William P. Alexander, of Springfield, Aids-de-camp.
Col. George H. Campbell, of Boston, Military Secretary.

FIRST BRIGADE MASSACHUSETTS VOLUNTEER MILITIA.

Brig.-Gen. Hobart Moore commanding.
American Band, of Boston.
Sixth Regiment of Infantry, Col. Melvin Beale commanding.
Fitchburg Brass Band.
Tenth Regiment of Infantry, Col. John W. Kimball commanding.
Mechanics' Band, of Orange.
Second Battalion of Infantry, Lieut.-Col. Robert J. Hamilton commanding.
American Band, of Providence.
Fourth Battalion of Infantry, Major Austin C. Wellington, Cambridge, commanding.
New Bedford Band.
Third Battalion of Infantry, Major Daniel A. Butler commanding.
Excelsior Band.
Unattached Company of Infantry, Boston, Captain C. F. A. Francis commanding.
Lawrence Brass Band.
First Battalion of Light Artillery, Major George S. Merrill commanding.
Dunstable Cornet Band.
Company F, Cavalry, Westford, Captain Sherman H. Fletcher.

SECOND BRIGADE MASSACHUSETTS VOLUNTEER MILITIA.

Brigadier-General Eben Sutton commanding.
Salem Band.
Eighth Regiment of Infantry, Colonel Benjamin F. Peach, Jr.
Fifth Regiment Band.
Fifth Regiment of Infantry, Colonel Ezra J. Trull, Boston.
Metropolitan Band.

Ninth Battalion of Infantry, Lieutenant-Colonel William M. Strachan, Boston.

Saunders' Band, of Peabody.

First Battalion of Infantry, Lieutenant-Colonel Nathaniel Wales, Boston.

Lynn Cornet Band.

Seventh Battalion of Infantry, Major Charles C. Fry, Lynn.

Battery A, Light Artillery, Boston, Captain Nathan Appleton.

Chelsea Cornet Band.

First Battalion of Cavalry, Major Dexter H. Follett, Boston.

FIRST DIVISION.

Gen. Horace Binney Sargent, Commander of the Department of Massachusetts Grand Army of the Republic, Chief of Division.

James F. Meech, Assistant Adjutant-General and Chief of Staff; Edward T. Raymond, Assistant Quartermaster-General; Frank H. Butler and W. H. Prescott, Color-Bearers; Cyrus C. Emery, John McKay, Jr., E. G. W. Cartwright, and Charles W. Wilcox, Council of Administration; Carriage containing Gen. John C. Robinson, U.S.A., Commander-in-Chief of the G.A.R.; J. F. Lovering, Chaplain-in-Chief; Stephen A. Oliver, National Aid-de-Camp, and Thomas Plunkett, Department Aid-de-Camp; Aids: Emerson Stone, D. H. L. Gleason, George H. Teague, G. A. Churchill, Charles H. Rust, W. H. Hildreth, George W. Creasey, W. H. Wade, C. W. C. Rhoades, Daniel D. Wiley, George P. Richardson, Charles H. Pinkham, Geo. E. Fayerweather, W. L. Coon, E. B. Putnam, Augustine Sanderson.

Shawmut Band.

THE GRAND ARMY OF THE REPUBLIC.

FIRST SUBDIVISION.

George S. Evans, Senior Vice-Commander of the Department of Massachusetts, in command.

W. W. Woodbury, Chief of Staff; William H. Cristie, Assistant Adjutant-General; Charles F. Allen, Assistant Quartermaster-General.
John Kinnear, Color-Bearer; Aids: A. R. Stover, Abner Coleman, Joseph O'Neill, E. A. Chandler, S. C. Barker, A. M. Tilton, Albert C. Andrew, William H. Eveleth.

Suffolk County.

Henry R. Sibley, of Boston, commanding.
Moncena Dunn, Assistant Adjutant-General and Chief of Staff.
E. M. Carey, Assistant Quartermaster-General.
G. W. Marsh, Color-Bearer.
Aids: Comrades Blood, Pease, Warner, Cushing, and Curry.
North Cambridge band.
Post No. 7 of Boston, John McDonough commanding.
Centennial Band, Portland.
Continental Drum Corps, Portland.
Post No. 2 of Portland, Me., Nathaniel Adams commanding.
Post No. 11 of Boston, Edmund C. Bradford commanding.
Post No. 15 of Boston, G. J. Hinds commanding.
Post No. 1 of Providence, R. I., C. H. Barney commanding.
Post No. 23 of East Boston, C. R. Roberts commanding.
Post No. 26 of Boston Highlands, Giles H. Rich commanding.
Post No. 32 of South Boston, S. B. Crane commanding.
Post No. 35 of Chelsea, C. F. Hodgkins commanding.
Post No. 68 of Boston, J. Beale commanding.
Post No. 92, M. Coyle, Jr., commanding.
Post No. 125 of South Boston, John A. Mackie commanding.
Post No. 134 of Boston, I. S. Mullen commanding.
Post No. 13, of Providence, R. I., D. E. Howard commanding.
Middlesex Band.
Post No. 149 of Boston, M. Donahue, commanding.

Plymouth County.

T. S. Atwood, of Abington, commanding.
E. A. Chase, Chief of Staff.

Charles D. Nash, Assistant Adjutant-General.
E. H. Atwood, Assistant Quartermaster-General.
John M. Penniman, Color-Bearer.
Aids: Alpheus Thomas, Joseph B. Chipman.
Bowles' South Abington Band.
Post No. 8, of Middleborough, A. W. Stoddard commanding.
Post No. 13, of Brockton, G. A. Grant commanding.
Post No. 31, of Scituate, Benjamin Brown commanding.
Post No. 73, of Abington, J. W. Sproul commanding.
Post No. 74, of Rockland, J. Looby commanding.
Post No. 76, of Plympton, F. M. Johnson commanding.
Post No. 78, of South Abington, A. C. Brigham commanding.
Post No. 83, of Hanover, M. V. Bonney commanding.
Post No. 104, of Hingham, Edwin Bouvé commanding.
Post No. 111, of Pembroke, H. C. Sampson commanding.
Post No. 112, of South Scituate, O. B. Prouty commanding.
Post No. 124, of East Bridgewater, L. F. Gammons commanding.
Post No. 127, of Hanson, J. G. Cook commanding.

Bristol County.

Edwin Dews, of New Bedford, commanding.
Henry A. Cushman, Chief of Staff.
W. Robert Williams, Assistant Adjutant-General.
Thomas J. Gifford, Assistant Quartermaster-General.
George E. Dean, Color-Bearer.
Aids: Frank McGraw, G. F. Fisher.
Post No. 1, New Bedford, W. G. Davis commanding.
Post No. 3, Taunton, Samuel K. Congdon commanding.
Post No. 46, Fall River, William O. Milne commanding.
Post No. 55, Taunton, Charles M. Cooley commanding.
Post No. 145, Attleborough, W. H. Goff commanding.
Post No. 146, New Bedford, George Delevan commanding.

Norfolk County.

G. Henry Perkins, of Hyde Park, commanding.
G. D. Willis, Chief of Staff.

J. B. Fisher, Assistant Adjutant-General.
William Emerson, Color-Bearer.
Hingham Band.
Simpson's Drum Corps.
Post No. 58, of Weymouth, B. S. Lowell commanding.
Post No. 72, of Stoughton, L. A. Thayer commanding.
Post No. 87, of Braintree, W. L. Gage commanding.
Post No. 88, of Quincy, S. B. Turner commanding.
Post No. 91, of Foxboro', J. S. Carver commanding.
Post No. 94, of Canton, A. A. Harrington commanding.
Post No. 105, of West Medway, D. S. Woodman commanding.
Post No. 110, of Randolph, Galen Hollis commanding.
Post No. 117, of Medfield, P. C. Grover commanding.
Post No. 121, of Hyde Park, R. F. Boynton commanding.
Post No. 143, of Brookline, W. B. Sears commanding.
Post No. 144, of Dedham, D. L. Hodges commanding.

Essex County.

Charles H. Chase, of Salem, commanding.
E. E. Austin, Assistant Adjutant-General and Chief of Staff.
E. L. Rowe, Assistant Quartermaster-General.
J. E. Trask, Color-Bearer.
Aids: H. G. Hyde, G. A. Andrews, W. T. Damon, H. H. Babb.
Lynn Drum Corps.
Post No. 5, of Lynn, A. J. Hoitt commanding.
Post No. 34, of Salem, W. H. Eastman commanding.
Lawrence Drum Corps.
Post No. 39, of Lawrence, D. F. Kiley commanding.
Post No. 45, of Gloucester, F. Locke, Jr., commanding.
Haverhill Drum Corps.
Post No. 47, of Haverhill, D. S. Kimball commanding.
Bailey's Band of Newburyport.
Post No. 49, of Newburyport, E. C. Pearson commanding.
Post No. 67, of Manchester, J. L. Eaton commanding.
Post No. 82, of Marblehead, J. S. Gregory commanding.

THE ARMY AND NAVY MONUMENT. 67

Beverly Band.
Post No. 89, of Beverly, H C. Woodbury commanding.
Danvers Drum Corps.
Post No. 90, of Danvers, Charles Newhall commanding.
Post No. 95, of Saugus, C. H. Mansfield commanding.
Post No. 100, of Methuen, R. H. Shiels commanding.
Groveland Band.
Post No. 101, of Groveland, L. H. Hopkinson commanding.
Post No. 108, of Georgetown, C. Gould commanding.
Post No. 114, of Merrimac, D. L. Getchell commanding.
Post No. 122, of Amesbury, J. O. Currier commanding.
Union Fife and Drum Corps of Peabody.
Post No. 132, of Peabody, J. R. Armstrong commanding.
Post No. 151, of West Newbury, O. Warren commanding.
Carriages containing Officers of the National Encampment, and the Departments of Maine, New Hampshire, and Rhode Island, and two hundred and forty wounded and disabled comrades, — all in charge of J. G. B. Adams, of the Council of Administration.

SECOND SUBDIVISION.

George H. Patch, Junior Vice-Commander of the Department of Massachusetts, in command.
M. B. Lakeman, Chief of Staff; H. C. Hall, Assistant Adjutant-General; George E. Priest, Assistant Quartermaster; Color-Bearer, J. W. Paine; Aids: J. M. Cate, E. P. Simpson, J. A. G. Richardson, L. V. Doane, R. F. Tobin, P. A. Lindsey, W. Livermore, J. T. Buffum, W. F. Wetherbee, L. J. Elwell.

Worcester County, with Posts from Hampden, Hampshire, Berkshire, and Franklin Counties attached.
William F. Draper, of Milford, commanding.
J. M. Drennan, Chief of Staff.
W. H. Scammell, Assistant Adjutant-General.
Lucius Fields, Assistant Quartermaster-General.
T. L. Ellsworth, Milford, Color-Bearer.

Milford Brass Band.
Johnson's Drum Corps, Worcester.
Post No. 10, Worcester, J. B. Lamb commanding.
Post No. 19, Fitchburg, James Daley commanding.
Post No. 22, Milford, H. J. Bailey commanding.
Post No. 24, Grafton, J. K. Axtell commanding.
Post No. 25, Uxbridge, E. J. Hill commanding.
Post No. 28, West Boylston, E. B. Berry commanding.
Post No. 37, Spencer, J. W. Bigelow commanding.
Drum Corps.
Post No. 38, Brookfield, A. D. Ward commanding.
Post No. 51, North Brookfield, S. E. Hoyt commanding.
Post No. 53, Leominster, C. A. Wheeler commanding.
Post No. 59, Sterling, G. F. Davidson commanding.
Post No. 61, Webster, Amos Bartlett commanding.
Drum Corps.
Post No. 64, Clinton, W. J. Coulter commanding.
Post No. 65, Warren, L. W. Gilbert commanding.
Post No. 69, Westminster, E. P. Miller commanding.
Drum Corps.
Post No. 70, Millbury, M. F. Bennett commanding.
Post No. 77, Holden, George Bascom commanding.
Post No. 96, Northboro', F. M. Harrington commanding.
Princeton Band.
Post No. 98, Princeton, E. E. Sawyer commanding.
Post No. 99, West Warren, H. L. Harmon commanding.
Post No. 116, South Gardner, E. P. Brown commanding.
Drum Corps.
Post No. 123, Athol, Charles Grey commanding.
Post No. 131, Leicester, G. F. Parker commanding.
Post No. 136, Rutland, C. H. Wesson commanding.
Drum Corps.
Post No. 16, Springfield, J. L. Knight commanding.
Post No. 17, Orange, R. W. Rand commanding.
Post No. 79, North Adams, W. W. Montgomery commanding.
Post No. 85, Ware, A. Warburton commanding,

THE ARMY AND NAVY MONUMENT. 69

Middlesex County.

George H. Copeland, of Cambridgeport, commanding; E. J. Dolan, Chief of Staff; Thomas E. Barker, Assistant Adjutant-General; J. W. Cummiskey, Assistant Quartermaster-General; John Kennady, Color-Bearer. Aids: Edward Niles, J. L. Keyser, G. W. Kent.

Natick Cornet Band.

Post No. 4, Melrose, M. S. Page commanding.
Post No. 6, Holliston, J. H. Osgood commanding.
Post No. 9, Hudson, E. P. Miles commanding.
Post No. 12, Wakefield, W. S. Greenough commanding.
Post No. 14, Woodville, Stephen Temple commanding.
Post No. 18, Ashland, Robert E. Gibson commanding.
Post No. 29, Waltham, Henry N. Fisher commanding.
Post No. 30, Cambridgeport, John B. Smithers commanding.
Post No. 33, Woburn, T. H. Hill commanding.
Post No. 40, Malden, G. W. McLaughlin commanding.
Post No. 42, Lowell, E. W. Thompson commanding.
Post No. 43, Marlboro', James L. Stone commanding.
Post No. 48, Ayer, Augustus Lovejoy commanding.

Townsend Band.

Post No. 50, Townsend, S. D. Hoyt commanding.
Post No. 56, of Cambridge, E. A. Stone commanding.
Post No. 57, East Cambridge, Geo. H. Howard commanding.
Post No. 62, Newton, T. Pickthall commanding.
Post No. 63, Natick, R. T. Nash commanding.
Post No. 66, Medford, J. E. Pierce commanding.
Post No. 75, Stoneham, M. J. Ferrin commanding.
Post No. 81, Watertown, Charles T. Perkins commanding.

Drum Corps.

Post No. 86, Maynard, E. E. Haynes commanding.
Post No. 115, Groton, M. P. Palmer commanding.
Post No. 139, Somerville, W. E. Halliday commanding.
Post No. 142, South Framingham, Geo. O. Bent commanding.
Post No. 148, Winchester, S. C. Small commanding.

SECOND DIVISION.

Colonel Edward O. Shepard, Chief of Division.

AIDS.

Major William P. Shreve, Assistant Adjutant-General; Major Edward P. Brown, Colonel George C. Joslin, Captain Fred. R. Shattuck, Colonel Solomon Hovey, Jr.

Waltham Band.
VETERANS OF MASSACHUSETTS.
Second Mass. Vol. Infantry, General George H. Gordon.
Sixth Mass. Vol. Infantry, Company K, Captain Walter S. Sampson.
Ninth Mass. Vol. Infantry, Major J. W. Mahan.
Twelfth Mass. Vol. Infantry, Lieutenant-Colonel B. F. Cook.
Newton Cornet Band.
Thirteenth Mass. Vol. Infantry, Colonel S. H. Leonard.
Twenty-first Mass. Vol. Infantry, Colonel George P. Hawkes.
Twenty-fourth Mass. Vol. Infantry, Colonel C. H. Hooper.
Twenty-eighth Mass. Vol. Infantry, Lieutenant Colonel J. McArdle.
Twenty-ninth Mass. Vol. Infantry, General Joseph H. Barnes.
Fortieth Mass. Vol. Infantry, Colonel Joseph A. Dalton.
Forty-second Mass. Vol. Infantry.
Forty-third Mass. Vol. Infantry, Colonel C. L. Holbrook.
Forty-fourth Mass. Vol. Infantry, Colonel E. C. Cabot.
Maplewood Band.
Forty-fifth Mass. Vol. Infantry, Lieutenant-Colonel Oliver W. Peabody.
Massachusetts Light Batteries, Colonel O. F. Nims.
Third Massachusetts Cavalry, Colonel L. D. Sargent.
N. P. Banks Army and Navy Association No. 1, Captain W. R. Riddle.
Wenham and Hamilton Veteran Association, Captain B. F. Young.
Reading Veteran Association, Captain W. W. Davis.
Naval Veteran Association, Captain George F. Hollis.
Hooker's Old Brigade (First Brigade, First Division, Third Army Corps), under command of General Gilman Marston.
First Regiment Band.
First Massachusetts Infantry, Lieutenant-Colonel C. B. Baldwin.

Eleventh Massachusetts Infantry, Lieutenant-Colonel C. C. Rivers.
Second New Hampshire Infantry, General J. N. Patterson,
Escorting Major General Joseph Hooker, U. S. A., and Reverend Warren H. Cudworth, Chaplain of the day.
New Hampshire War Veterans, General A. F. Stevens.
Maine Veterans in Massachusetts, Colonel William Gillispie.
Army of the Tennessee Association.
Ninety-ninth New York Infantry, General D. W. Wardrop.
Newport and Rhode Island Veterans, Captain Andrew McMahon.
Survivors of Rebel Prisons, Colonel John Read.
Disabled Veterans in Barges.

THIRD DIVISION.

Colonel Charles E. Fuller, Chief of Division.

AIDS.

Captain James Thompson, Assistant Adjutant-General; Mr. S. D. Warren, Jr., Captain R. C. Downer, Mr. E. T. Hastings, Mr. F. H. Babson.

Fall River Band.
Boston School Regiment, Lieutenant-Colonel George W. Forristall commanding.
Barge, drawn by six bay horses, containing young ladies of the public schools, representing the Goddess of Liberty and the States of the Union, in charge of Mr. G. B. Putnam, Master of Franklin School.

The young ladies were dressed in white, with a sash of red, white, and blue silk, and wore very pretty turban caps, composed of the national colors, and each carried a banneret with the name of the State she represented. The seats were arranged in tiers, with a central dais for the young lady representing the Goddess of Liberty. She was dressed in white, and wore a sash like the rest, but instead of a banner she supported a handsome American flag, and wore a Liberty Cap. At the head of the barge was a blue silk banner, upon which, in letters of gold, were: —

"𝕿𝖍𝖊 𝕾𝖎𝖘𝖙𝖊𝖗 𝕾𝖙𝖆𝖙𝖊𝖘, 𝖂𝖊 𝕳𝖔𝖓𝖔𝖗 𝕿𝖍𝖊 𝕳𝖊𝖗𝖔𝖎𝖈 𝕯𝖊𝖆𝖉."

Bond's Brigade Band, mounted.
Prescott Guards, Captain Freeman L. Gilman commanding.
Carriage containing Major-General George B. McClellan, Colonel Edward H. Wright, of New Jersey, and Colonel Henry Walker, Aid to the Chief Marshal.
Manchester Cadets, of Manchester, N. H., Captain F. H. Challis commanding.

FOURTH DIVISION.

Major J. Henry Sleeper, Chief of Division.

AIDS.

Major Cyrus S. Haldeman, Captain N. T. Apollonio, Lieutenant Charles Fairchild, Captain Joseph H. Lathrop, Captain W. W. Carruth.

Colt's Armory Band.
United States Marine Corps, and detachment of United States Sailors, with howitzers, Colonel James Jones commanding,
Escorting the City Government and Invited Guests.
Alderman Charles W. Wilder, Councilmen Lowell B. Hiscock, James J. Flynn, and James H. Nugent, of the Committee on Army and Navy Monument, mounted.
Carriages containing the Honorable Frederick O. Prince, Mayor; Alderman Francis Thompson, Chairman Monument Committee; Alvah H. Peters, City Messenger.
Alderman John T. Clark, Chairman of the Board of Aldermen; Martin Milmore, Designer and Sculptor of the Monument.
Members of the Board of Aldermen.
Members of the Common Council.

The Massachusetts Commandery of the Military Order of the Loyal
Legion of the United States, under the command of
General Alfred P. Rockwell,
Escorting
Honorable CHARLES DEVENS, the Orator of the Day,
and
General Francis A. Osborn, Past Commander of the Commandery.

Carriages with invited guests, as follows: —

Commodore Foxhall A. Parker, and Officers attached to the Navy Yard
at Charlestown.
General Thomas Wilson, Colonel C. L. Best, Major A. G. Robinson,
and Captain Cullen Bryant.
Lieutenant R. H. Patterson.
Officers of the U. S. Revenue Steamers "Gallatin" and "H. Hamlin."
The Hon. Horatio G. Knight, Lieutenant-Governor of Massachusetts.
The Hon. Joseph K. Baker, the Hon. Harrison Tweed, the Hon. Francis
Childs, the Hon. Hugh J. Toland.
The Hon. William Cogswell, the Hon. Joseph A. Harwood, the Hon.
George Whitney, and the Hon. William C. Plunkett,
members of the Executive Council.
The Hon. N. P. Banks, the Hon. William Claflin, the Hon. W. A. Field,
and the Hon. Leopold Morse, members of Congress.
The Hon. J. B. D. Cogswell, President of the Massachusetts Senate;
the Hon. John D. Long, Speaker of the Massachusetts
House of Representatives.
The Hon. Josiah Quincy and Major-General J. M. Schofield.
The Hon. Joseph M. Wightman and Major-General C. C. Augur and
Aids.
Major-General S. P. Heintzelman, Major-General T. W. Sherman, and
Major-General John C. Robinson.
General John G. Barnard, General Z. B. Tower, and General Q. A.
Gilmore.
Hon. Henry L. Pierce, General J. L. Chamberlain, and General D. N.
Couch.

General M. T. McMahon, and General William Raymond Lee.
General G. K. Warren, and General John M. Corse.
General E. W. Hinks, General Rufus Saxton, and General A. B. Underwood.
Jarvis D. Braman, Colonel T. Y. Simons, and General Lucius H. Warren.
General W. W. Averill, General Charles Herring, and Theodore McIntire.
M. F. Dickinson, John J. McNutt, Admiral Charles Steedman, and Commodore W. H. Shock.
Surgeon-General William Greer and Commodore W. A. Nicholson.
Hiram A. Wright, Joseph Story, Francis W. Pray, and Clement H. Hill.
Hon. William Gaston, Hon. Richard Frothingham, Hon. George A. Shaw, and Hon. T. J. Dacey.
Matthias Rich and Joel Seaverns, M.D.
Hon. Frank A. Allen, Mayor of Cambridge; Hon. Austin Belknap, Mayor of Somerville; and Hon. Alden Speare, Mayor of Newton.
Hon. W. A. Simmons, Collector of the Port of Boston; Hon. E. S. Tobey, Postmaster; and Roland G. Usher, United States Marshal.
The Hon. Joseph F. Paul, President of the Massachusetts Charitable Mechanic Association; J. D. Runkle, President of the Institute of Technology; the Hon. J. W. Candler, President of the Board of Trade; Hon. Marshall P. Wilder, President of the N. E. Historic-Genealogical Society.
Veterans of the War of 1812: the Hon. Charles Hudson, Col. Henry Little, William Goodwin, John Wright, Joseph Sanderson, George Hooper, William Dewing, Daniel Simpson.
Officers of the Massachusetts Volunteers in Mexico: Col. Isaac H. Wright, Capt. William Hurd, Henry A. M'Glenen, S. L. Page.
Members of the Board of Directors for Public Institutions.
Joseph Smith, Gen Isaac S. Burrill, Colonel W. H. McCauley, and Colonel J. W. Gilray.
The Hon. Thomas Russell, Samuel A. Green, M.D., John F. Andrew, George F. Babbitt, and the Rev. George E. Ellis, D.D.
C. L. Flint, Martin Beatty, John C. Crowley, Joseph Burnett, Professor Owen, William M. Meehan, and Robert D. Joyce, M.D.

FIFTH DIVISION.

General Samuel C. Lawrence, Chief of Division.

AIDS.

Major G. O. Carpenter, Assistant Adjutant General; Thomas B. Jordan, Maj. Charles W. Stevens, William H. Guild, Corliss Wadleigh.

FIRST SUBDIVISION.

Brown's Brigade Band.
The Grand Commandery of Knights Templars, of Massachusetts and Rhode Island, with its subordinate Commanderies.
Carriages containing Right Eminent Grand Commander Henry W. Rugg, with his guests, including Very Eminent Grand Generalissimo of the Grand Encampment of the United States, Benjamin Dean; Very Eminent Sir S. R. Sircum, Past Grand Provincial Prior of the Great Canadian Priory; Very Eminent Sir John Dean, Deputy Grand Commander of the Grand Commandery of Massachusetts; Past Grand Commander Nicholas Van Slyck; Past Grand Commander James Hutchinson; Grand Capt.-Gen. of the Grand Commandery of Massachusetts, George E. Stacy; Past Grand Generalissimo of the Grand Encampment of Massachusetts, William B. Blandin, and others of eminence in the order.

Nelson W. Aldrich, Generalissimo.

AIDS.

Eminent Sirs Henry A. Pierce, John Kent, and Erastus H. Doolittle, and Sir William R. Walker.

Pawtucket Band.
Saint John's Commandery of Providence, R. I., George H. Burnham, Eminent Commander.
Worcester Brass Band.
Worcester County Commandery, of Worcester, David F. Parker, Eminent Commander.

American Brass Band.
Pilgrim Commandery, of Lowell, John M. Pevey, Eminent
Commander.
Maitland's Band of Brockton.
Palestine Commandery, of Chelsea, John C. Hall, Eminent
Commander.
Wakefield Brass Band.
Hugh de Payens Commandery, of Melrose, James Swords,
Eminent Commander.
Brown's Brigade Band, Boston.
St. Omer Commandery, South Boston, Benjamin Pope, Eminent
Commander.
Woonsocket Brass Band.
Woonsocket Commandery of Woonsocket, R. I., E. Aldrich,
Eminent Commander.
Connecticut Valley Commandery, Greenfield, Marvin S. Fellows,
Eminent Commander.
Mansfield Brass Band.
William Parkman Commandery, East Boston, William Waters,
Eminent Commander.
Marlborough Brass Band.
Trinity Commandery of Hudson, James L. Harriman, Eminent
Commander.
Weymouth Brass Band.
South Shore Commandery, Weymouth, William Humphreys,
Eminent Commander.
Edmands' Band.
Cœur de Lion Commandery, of Boston, John B. Wilson, Eminent
Commander.
South Easton Brass Band.
Bay State Commandery, Brockton, B. Sanford, Eminent
Commander.
Calvary Commandery, of Providence, R. I., mounted. James
G. Stiness, Acting Commander.
Carter's Band.
Boston Commandery, Samuel Mason, Jr., Eminent Commander,

225 Knights, acting as special Guard of Honor to the
M.W. Grand Lodge of Massachusetts.
M.W. Percival Lowell Everett, G.M.
R.W. Charles A. Welch, D.G.M.
R.W. Daniel W. Lawrence, S.G.W.
R.W. Edward Avery, J.G.W.
R.W. John McClellan, G.T.
R.W. Charles H. Titus, R.G.S.
R.W. George P. Sanger, C.G.S.

District Deputy Grand Masters: R.W. Seth C. Ames, R.W. Edward C. Damon, R.W. William C. Maxwell, R.W. Warren Currier, R.W. Solon W. Stevens, R.W. Henry M. Humphrey, R.W. John A. Hall, R.W. Charles W. Moody, R.W. Irving B. Sayles, R.W. Frederick D. Ely, R.W. Abraham G. Hart, R. W. Russell Matthews, R.W. Hosea Kingman, R.W. Theodore N. Foque.

Grand Chaplains: W. Rev. Alonzo H. Quint, D.D., W. Rev. Joshua Young.

Grand Marshal: W. William H. Chessman.

Grand Lecturers: W. Thomas Waterman, W. Charles M. Avery.

W. William H. H. Soule, S.G.D.; W. Charles E. Smith, J.G.D.

W. Marlborough Williams, S.G.S.

W. Thomas Davis, W. Henry Stephenson, J.G.S.

Grand Standard Bearer: W. Z. L. Bicknell.

Grand Pursuivant: W. Henry S. Bunton.

Grand Tyler: Bro. Benjamin F. Nourse.

Past Grand Masters: R.W. John T. Heard, R.W. William D. Coolidge, R.W. William Parkman, R.W. Charles C. Dame,
R.W. Sereno D. Nickerson.

P.D.G. Masters: R.W. Rev. E. M. P. Wells, R.W. G. Washington Warren.

P.G. Wardens: R.W. Henry Chickering, R.W. William W. Baker, R.W. William Sutton, R.W. Samuel P. Oliver, R.W. William F. Salmon, R.W. Samuel C. Lawrence, R.W. Charles Kimball, R.W. Henry Endicott, R.W. Abraham H. Howland, Jr., R.W. Peter C. Jones, R.W. Wyzeman Marshall,

R.W. Ivory H. Pope, R.W. Elijah W. Burr, R.
W. Tracy P. Cheever, R.W. Charles G.
Reed, R.W. Lucius W. Lovell.

Brethren present as guests of the Grand Lodge: —

M.W. Edward P. Burnham, Grand Master of Masons in Maine.
M.W. Charles R. Cutler, Grand Master of Masons in Rhode Island.
R.W. Thomas A. Doyle, Past Grand Master of the Grand Lodge of
Rhode Island.
R.W. Clinton F. Paige, Past Grand Master of the Grand Lodge of
New York.
W. Albert P. Moriarty, Past Grand Deacon of the Grand Lodge of
New York.

SECOND SUBDIVISION.

The Patriarchal Branch of the Independent Order of Odd Fellows of
Massachusetts.
Samuel B. Krogman, Marshal.

STAFF.

William M. Rumery, Chief of Staff.
E. H. Adams, Assistant Adjutant-General.

AIDS.

Samuel Shaw, George T. Wade, Thomas H. Burgess, Samuel Cochran,
F. A. Whitmore, Edward M. Rumery, Frank M. Babcock.

Fall River Brass Band.
Regiment of Massachusetts Encampments: Col. James W. Chapman,
Lieut.-Col. Irving Jones, Maj. William F. Gardner,
Adj. S. L. Hodges, Surg. Dr. George S. Jones,
Quartermaster George H. Ellis.
Massasoit Encampment, No. 1 (four companies); Charles H. Porter,
Captain First Company; John P. Wild, Captain Second Company; A. Masters, Jr., Captain Third Company;
George H. Leach, Captain Fourth Company.

Mount Washington Encampment, No. 6 (two companies): Charles
Turpin, Captain Fifth Company; John B. Hughes,
Captain Sixth Company.
Boston Encampment, No. 38 (two companies): A. G. W. Cates, Captain Seventh Company; F. R. A. Pingree, Captain Eighth Company.
Trimount Encampment, No. 2, of Boston (two companies):
A. L. Sanborn, Captain Ninth Company; Thomas N.
Cook, Jr., Captain Tenth Company.
Winthrop Brass Band.
Nemasket Encampment, No. 44, John O. Emerson commanding.
Officers of the Grand Encampment in carriages.
Lafayette Marshal, M.W. Grand Patriarch; Nathaniel A. Very, M.E.
Grand High Priest; John J. Whipple, R.W. Grand Senior
Warden; Charles D. Cole, R. W. Grand Scribe; William
D. Hay, R.W. Grand Junior Warden; E. Bently
Young, W. Grand Instructor; and Charles Hayden and Jonathan Livermore, Past Grand
Patriarchs.

Officers of the Grand Lodge in carriages.
John U. Perkins, M.W. Grand Master; Albert L. Fessenden, R.W.
Deputy Grand Master; William W. Gardner, R.W. Grand Warden;
Eugene F. Endicott, W. Grand Marshal; Edwin L. Pilsbury,
W. Grand Conductor; Nathaniel Adams, William E.
Ford, Levi F. Warren, George B. Hamlin, and Fred
C. Davis, Past Grand Masters.

THIRD SUBDIVISION.

The Order of Knights of Pythias of Massachusetts,
Samuel M. Weale, Grand Chancellor, commanding.
Aids: A. M. Parker, Assistant Adjutant-General; Henry F. Spach,
Chief of Staff; George E. Filkins, Joseph F. French.
Henry Thurston, Color Bearer.

Randolph Brass Band.
Braintree Drum Corps.

FIRST DIVISION.

William H. Lee, Grand Vice-Chancellor, commanding.

AIDS.

H. V. Hayward, William Tyner.

Delphi Lodge, No. 15, of Weymouth, G. P. Lyons, Commander.
Palestine Lodge, No. 26, of Haverhill, C. W. Bradley, Commander.
Boston Lodge, No. 3, A. T. Merrill, Commander.
Trimountain Lodge, No. 6, of Boston, R. Landry, Commander.
Washington Lodge, No. 10, P. M. Foss, Commander.
Socrates Lodge, No. 21, Robert Luscomb commanding.
Unity Lodge, No. 44, Edmund Parkman commanding.
Ivanhoe Lodge, No. 13.
Officers and invited guests in carriages, including S. S. Davis, Nashua, N. H., Supreme Chancellor; F. A. Chase, G.K.R.S.; L. M. T. Hill, G.P.; W. L. Mallery, P.C., Glenn's Falls, N. Y.

SECOND DIVISION.

Edwin R. Young, G. Master of Exchequer, commanding.

AIDS.

Joseph A. Hoyt, C. H. Thrasher, Samuel I. Segar.

French's Cornet Band.
Blake Lodge, No. 49, and Damascus Lodge, No. 50, of Worcester, consolidated, F. E. Hall, Commander.
Lyman Drum Corps.
Calanthe Lodge, No. 17, of Lynn, John S. Tarr, Commander.
King Philip Lodge, No. 33, of East Boston, J. M. Prior, Commander.
Maverick Lodge, No. 39, of East Boston, C. E. Leavitt, Commander.
Massachusetts Lodge, No. 42, and Teutonic Lodge, No. 47, of Boston Highlands, Thomas P. Sweat, Commander.
Mystic Lodge, No. 46, of Chelsea, William H. Cate, Jr., Commander.

SIXTH DIVISION.

Colonel A. Parker Browne, Chief of Division.

AIDS.

Lieutenant Charles A. Campbell, Assistant Adjutant-General; Captain Daniel H. Johnson, Lieutenant George T. Browne, Dr. Arthur Kemble.

Belknap Band.
Temple of Honor of Massachusetts.
Chief Marshal, Joseph Austin; Chief of Staff, H. W. Woodbury; Adjutant, O. Lawrence; Sergeant-Major, Fred A. Waitt.

AIDS.

W. B. Reed, D. S. Gammon, D. R. Morrill, F. W. Peak, T. B. Campbell, William Horton, D. P. Lincoln, R. W. Chandler, J. B. Brown, Thomas Real, H. W. Wilson, W. H. Craven, J. W. Follett, John Prince, A. E. Worthen, B. F. Allen, W. J. Dunbar.
Howard Temple, No. 10, Lynn, B. P. Boynton, Marshal.
Trimount Temple, No. 1, Boston, D. S. McGregor, Marshal.
Mechanics' Temple, No. 25, East Weymouth.
Temple Drum Corps, escorting
Select Templars of Honor, J. B. Brown, Marshal.
Carriages containing G.W. Templar A. H. Lewis; G.W.V. Templar George W. Dyer; G.W. Recorder Walter Babb; G.W. Treasurer J. W. Bailey; M.W. Recorder R. C. Bull, and Grand Chief of Council John G. Brayman.
Mt. Sinai Temple, No. 14, Chelsea, T. B. Campbell, Marshal.
Neptune Temple, No. 26, Gloucester, Charles Andrews, Marshal.
Atlantic Temple, No. 49, East Gloucester, Alexander Griswold, Marshal.
Fidelity Temple, No. 6, Lawrence, J. H. Morgan, Marshal.
Good Will Temple, No. 32, Waltham, J. O. Winn, Marshal.

Massasoit Temple, No. 46, Springfield ; Worcester, No. 31, Worcester ;
Olive Branch, No. 38, Worcester ; Monadnock, No. 17,
Fitchburg ; Jerusalem, No. 45, Holyoke,
J. A. French, Marshal.
St. Paul's Temple, No. 41, East Somerville ; St. Mark's, No. 23,
Fall River, George B. Parsons, Marshal.
St. John's Temple, No. 30, Boston ; Bunker Hill, No. 11, Charlestown ;
Mount Lebanon, No. 4, Medford ; Fraternity, No. 2, Boston,
J. H. Brown, Marshal.

Belknap Band of Quincy.
Grand Division Sons of Temperance of Massachusetts, in 15 carriages ;
the Rev. E. S. Potter, G.W.P. ; B. R. Jewell, G.T. ;
Jonathan Butterfield, P.G.W.P. ; S. W. Hodges,
M.W.S. ; Andrew M. Eastman, P.G.W.A. ;
H. H. Sullivan, G.D.Pr.

National Band of Boston.
Col. Laing and Staff of the Seventy-ninth New York Highlanders, in full
Scottish dress, as guests of the Caledonia Club, — Captain
Joseph Ross, Captain William Lindsey, Captain
Donald Cameron, Captain David E. Vannett.

Boston Caledonia Club, in Highland costume, William Grant, Chief,
Escorting the Scots' Charitable Society, Alexander D. Sinclair, President, under command of J. Stuart
McCorry, Marshal.

Carriages containing distinguished members of the Scottish Clubs,
David Thompson, James B. Hill, James Cruikshanks.

Ripley's Brass Band of Boston.
Portuguese Benevolent Society, Marshal, John Louis Almeida.

Polish Kosciusko Society, L. K. Noversky, President.

Hibernia Brass Band of Natick.
Journeymen Horseshoers' Mutual Relief Society, Marshal, John Rooney.

SEVENTH DIVISION.

Colonel Patrick T. Hanley, Chief of Division.

AIDS.

Major Daniel G. McNamara, Assistant Adjutant-General; Captain Christopher Plunkett, Captain James Dowling, Captain Joseph T. Ryan, J. W. Hanlon, Major P. E. Murphy.

Brookline Band.
Knights of St. Patrick, Captain Martin Fay commanding.
Barouche containing Rev. J. B. Donegan, of Marlborough, Chaplain of the organization.

FIRST SUBDIVISION.

Marshal, Timothy Deasey.

AIDS.

Major L. J. Logan, John Miller, P. Greeley, and John Scully.

Officers of Convention of Irish Societies of Boston, in barouches.
President, Edward Riley.
American Band of Cambridge.
American Society of Hibernians of South Boston, Andrew Strain commanding, with barouche containing officers of the organization.
Charlestown City Band.
Division No. 7, Ancient Order Hibernians of Milford, Mass., James F. Stratton commanding.
Ancient Order of Hibernians of Mass.; Grand State Delegate William H. Cook, John Dolan, State Secretary, and M. J. Callahan, Treasurer, in barouche.
Mounted escort of 20 men from Divisions 1, 2 and 3, A.O.H., Boston, M. H. Reddish commanding.
Division 1, A.O.H., M. F. Rowen commanding, with two barouches.

Division 2, A.O.H., Boston, John C. McDevitt, with two barouches.
Division 3, A.O.H., Boston Highlands, George F. Ballou commanding.
Division 4, A.O.H., Boston, with barouche,
James Conboy commanding.
Union Band of Brockton.
Division 1, A.O.H., of Brockton, Patrick Gilmore commanding.
Division 5, Charlestown, James Towle commanding.
Division 6, A.O.H., South Boston, barouche, Robert Johnson commanding.
Division 7, A.O.H., South Boston, J. P. Connor commanding.
Division 9, A.O.H., Boston Highlands, James J. Lynch commanding.
Ayer Cornet Band.
Division 7, A.O.H., of Ayer, M. Rynn commanding.
Division 2, A.O.H., of Lowell, John J. Mealy commanding.
Division 11, A.O.H., of Lowell, J. F. Convery commanding.
Division 4, A.O.H., of Stoneham, John McDonald commanding.
Division 4, A.O.H., of Quincy, P. F. Lacey commanding.
Drum Corps.
Division 5, A.O.H., of Cambridgeport, Peter F. O'Rourke commanding.
Division 15, A.O.H., of Cambridge, John McSorley commanding.
Boardman's Drum Corps, of Waltham.
Division 19, A.O.H., of Waltham, Edward Kenneally commanding, with barouche containing officers.
Division 18, A.O.H., of East Woburn, William McDonough commanding.
Division 26, A.O.H., of Wakefield, C. F. Doherty commanding.
Ashland Drum Corps.
Division 22, A.O.H., of Ashland, John O'Brien commanding.
Natick Drum Corps.
Division 27, A.O.H., of Natick, D. Greene commanding.
Westborough Cornet Band.
Division 20, A.O.H., of Westborough, D. D. Dirnan commanding.
Division 12, A.O.H., of Southbridge, James Morrissey commanding.
Division 21, A.O.H., of Worcester, barouche,
E. McHugh commanding.

SECOND SUBDIVISION.

Chief Marshal, P. H. Barry.

AIDS.

E. J. Flaherty, Chief of Staff; Hugh McGarvey, T. J. Dunn, F. J. McGrath, John R. Kennedy, Frank McCarthy, John Doolin, Thomas McCullough, John J. Connolly, Dennis Barry, Jeremiah Murphy. Michael Riley, John Reardon, Charles Haney, Daniel Sheehy, P. H. Shea, John F. Daley, Timothy J. Wallace, William Lynch.

Suffolk County Division of the Massachusetts Catholic Total Abstinence Union.

Medway Cornet Band.

Father Mathew T.A. Society, No. 2, P. J. Smith commanding.

SS. Peter and Paul T.A. Society, South Boston, James Sheridan commanding.

South Boston Y.M.T.A. Society, J. J. Prendergrast commanding.

St. Augustine's (senior society), South Boston, with officers in barouche, Patrick Kane, Marshal, commanding.

St. Augustine Young Men's Society, J. J. Murphy, Commander.

St. Stephen's Band.

St. Stephen's T.A. Society, Cornelius Desmond, Commander, with officers in carriages.

St. Stephen's Guard of Honor Cadets, James Folan, Commander.

St. Rose T.A.B. Society of Chelsea, Dennis Kelleher, Commander, with officers in barouche.

Needham Brass Band.

St. James Young Men's Total Abstinence Society of Boston, with Drum Corps, 8 pieces, P. J. O'Brien, Marshal, with barouche containing officers.

St. Valentine's Drum Corps.

St. Valentine's T.A.B. Society, under Dennis Shea, with two barouches containing officers.

This division closed the procession.

The total number of men in the procession, according to the consolidated reports, was 25,429, and the time occupied in passing a given point (all delays being deducted) was about four hours.

The route was $6\frac{1}{10}$ miles in length.

After the Chief Marshal had passed the State House, the First Corps of Cadets wheeled out of the column and drew up on each side of the main entrance. The Commander-in-Chief and Staff halted upon the sidewalk in front of the gate and reviewed the militia and veteran divisions. The Chief Marshal reviewed the procession at the corner of Charles and Beacon streets.

Many interesting mementos of the war were carried in the procession.

The Chief Marshal's flag was the same which marked his headquarters when commanding artillery, in the Fifth Army Corps. The Second Massachusetts Veterans carried a regimental flag made by the loyal ladies of Harper's Ferry, and which was carried through the battles of Newton, Winchester, Cedar Mountain, and Antietam. Co. K, of the Sixth Massachusetts, carried a flag presented to the regiment by the ladies of Baltimore. The Ninth Regiment carried a flag presented by the boys of the Eliot School. It was carried by John F. Donovan, who took the flag on the first of July, 1863, in the Seven Days' Fight, after eight men had been killed under it, and who was badly wounded while carrying it in this fight. The Twelfth Regiment carried the remnants of the old regimental flag. The horse ridden through the war by Quartermaster George E. Mussey, appeared with this regiment. The Thirteenth Regiment carried the old brigade flag, which had been borne through the Second Bull Run fight, and from that time in every engagement in which the regiment participated. The Twenty-first Regiment carried the remnants of their old battle-flag. The First Battery carried the spear-head and tassels, all that remained of the battery flag, and the guidon which was carried to the war. The Fifth Battery carried its old flag. The

Fourth Battery carried the first guidon taken by the battery. The Third Massachusetts Cavalry carried its old regimental colors. At the head of the First Massachusetts Regiment was borne the original battle-flag of Hooker's Old Brigade. The Maine Veteran Association carried the colors of the Third Maine Regiment. At the head of a platoon of Post 75 G.A.R. was Peter Nolan, a comrade of the Post, who marched over the entire route on crutches, having lost a leg at the second battle of Bull Run.

THE DEDICATION.

THE DEDICATION.

The dedicatory ceremonies were held on a platform erected at the base and on the south side of the Monument.

This platform covered an area of 15,000 square feet, and accommodated 3,200 spectators with seats. It was divided into sections, which were lettered, to avoid confusion, and to which admission was gained by tickets correspondingly lettered.

The seats were in charge of the following corps of ushers: —

Chief Usher, EUGENE FOSTER.

AIDS.

W. L. Wilder,	J. W. Warren,	W. B. White,
John Shepard, Jr.	Wm. F. Andrews, Jr.	J. B. Williams,
Joseph N. Baxter,	F. W. Ruggles,	G. C. Kingsbury,
J. J. O'Reagan,	S. H. Gardner,	Ivory Bean, Jr.

The speaker's table was on the west side of the platform, and the Masonic table was immediately in front of the Monument.

The City Government, invited guests, and Grand Lodge of Masons arrived at the platform at twenty minutes past five o'clock, and the ceremonies of dedication were opened with the performance of Keller's American Hymn, by Colt's Armory Band, under the direction of J. Thomas Baldwin. At the conclusion of the hymn the Hon. Francis Thompson, Chairman of the Committee on Army and Navy Monument, introduced the

Rev. WARREN H. CUDWORTH, the Chaplain of the Day, who offered the following prayer: —

PRAYER OF REV. WARREN H. CUDWORTH, CHAPLAIN OF THE DAY.

Almighty Maker of the heavens and the earth, who hast created the members of Thy human family in Thine own image, and crowned them with glory and honor, we desire to thank Thee that among the nations gathered providentially upon the face of the earth to settle and subdue it, our free American nation has in these times found her place and commenced her work. We thank Thee, that although that place was fiercely shaken, and that work temporarily interrupted by the four great wars which have raged within our borders or along our shores since the commencement of our national career, Thine arm has been stretched out always to rescue us from threatened destruction, and Thy favor has inspired our people, on mountain and plain, on lake and river, on sea and land, to the repeated and faithful discharge of their duty in the hour of danger.

We would especially adore Thee, that upon the termination of the recent disastrous and deplorable civil war, our country, although weak and trembling on account of the fury of the storm which had swept over her, still retained her freedom and her unity; her unbroken territorial proportions; her instinctive reverence for the laws of God; her sublime devotion to the rights of man; without a star stricken from her banner, or a stain left upon her escutcheon.

Aid us, we pray Thee, to recognize with a profound feeling of patriotic gratitude and tender affection, the obligations we are under to those noble and heroic men, living and dead, who, upon so many hard-fought battle-fields, at the post of duty on the decks of so many war-ships, in trench, redoubt, and fort, on picket, on the watch, in captivity, or in the hospital, bravely withstood the shock of conflict, or patiently endured wounds, sickness, and death, that we, and all generations to come, might inherit union and liberty throughout the land.

May we realize to-day, may we nevermore forget, that the institutions which enrich, adorn, and dignify us as a nation have cost hunger and thirst, weariness and pain, privation and peril, sorrow, suffering, life and limb to hundreds of thousands of our fellow-countrymen, and thus learn to appreciate their value, and resolve to secure their perpetuity for all coming time.

Accept, O God, the solemn act of consecration, which has gathered together in this historic place so vast a concourse of Thy children, that they may suitably dedicate and set apart the memorial column which towers above them to the grand and appropriate mission for which it was designed. May its fair and harmonious proportions, its silent but symbolic figures, its expressive carvings and bas-reliefs, its touching records of the heroism, the fortitude, the self-sacrifice of those to whose remembrance it has been erected, never fail to awaken in all beholders feelings of profound reverence for the God of nations, and of heartfelt gratitude to the brave and gallant dead, who, beneath the sod of so many battle-fields, and under the waters washing so many shores, found honorable graves in maintaining the integrity of their country. May it recall the valor, the fortitude, the devotion to duty, which nerved officers and men throughout the army and navy during the war for the preservation of our national union, and inspire all who gaze upon it with a lively appreciation of their labors, sufferings, and sacrifices, and an earnest determination to cultivate the same virtues, and exhibit the same spirit for the good of others, in their own day and generation.

Crown with speedy and enduring success, we beseech Thee, the efforts specially put forth at this time, throughout the land, to heal the wounds and remove the bitterness caused by our recent sad and sanguinary war. Restore harmony and good feeling to all those who have been discordant and inimical; and hasten the happy period when the separate States of this great country, North and South, East and West, united and accordant, shall march on with undivided and unbroken front to the accomplishment of the great end for which we have been providentially called into being as a nation.

Cheer and sustain the bereaved households, the afflicted relatives and friends of our gallant and patriotic dead, throughout the land, and strengthen them from above to endure submissively the bereavement which has separated them from husbands, fathers, sons, and brothers on earth, in the hope of a blessed reunion in heaven, where the pain of parting is never felt.

Bless the efforts which wise and Christian philanthropists are making everywhere to obviate the necessity and stay the ravages of warfare among the nations of the earth; and speed the time when men shall beat their swords into ploughshares, their spears into pruning-hooks, and throughout all lands, across all waters, peace shall everywhere prevail and good-will towards mankind become the most prominent and powerful characteristic of all human dealings and relationships, both national and individual.

Command Thy blessing, O Lord, upon those who participate in these services to-day; upon the sculptor, whose finished and beautiful work we unfold to the observation of mankind; upon our honored guests from other places; upon the speaker who shall address us from this platform; upon the official representatives of our army and navy, present and past; upon the various organizations, civil and military, of our fellow-countrymen, who have appeared in the procession and taken part in the proceedings of this commemorative occasion; upon the President of the United States, the Governors of the various States, and their associates in official station; upon the Mayor and other officers connected with the City Government of Boston; upon the special committee on the Army and Navy Monument, to whose unremitting labor and comprehensive oversight we owe so much of the happiness of this hour; upon all the people of this city, this country, and the world; and grant, O most gracious Creator, that our nation, our State, our own municipality, may never lack the men needed to stand by the great principles of freedom, of union, and of universal human equality before the law; the men needed, perchance, like the honored dead this day commemorated, to suffer and die for the maintenance of these principles in their own day, and their transmission to posterity.

And unto Thee, O God, our heavenly Father, we will forever give all the praise and glory, through Thy Son, our Saviour, Jesus Christ. Amen.

At the conclusion of the prayer, the Sculptor, MARTIN MILMORE, surrendered the Monument, in the following words: —

Mr. Chairman and Gentlemen of the Committee, — The work which the city entrusted to me is finished, and is here submitted for your approval and acceptance. I have endeavored to execute a fitting memorial to the men of Boston, who died that the nation might live. Whether I have succeeded in giving adequate expression to the gratitude of the people it is for you, as their representatives, to say. I have to thank you, gentlemen, and your predecessors in office, for the generous support which I have received during the progress of the work.

Alderman THOMPSON responded as follows: —

Mr. Milmore, — In behalf of the Committee of the City Council to whom was assigned the charge of the Army and Navy Monument, I desire to say that, as you well know, they have carefully watched the progress of the work; they believe that you have faithfully and honestly complied with the terms of your contract, and I am authorized in their behalf to accept the Monument.

Alderman THOMPSON then requested M.W. PERCIVAL L. EVERETT, Grand Master, to dedicate the Monument, in the following words: —

Most Worshipful Grand Master of the Grand Lodge of Massachusetts, — Six years ago at this time the corner-stone of yonder Monument was laid with imposing ceremonies by the Grand Lodge of Massachusetts. In the mean time the Monument has been constructed, and now the designer and builder surrenders it to the city as completed. The committee in charge were desirous it should receive the Masonic ceremonies of dedication, agreeably to ancient custom, and respectfully invited you and your fraternity to be present on this occasion.

Permit me, in behalf of the committee, to thank you, sir, and your fraternity, for the noble manner in which you have responded to the call, by the full attendance of the brethren of the Order. I have now to request that you will perform, as far as the limited time will permit, those services according to Masonic usages.

The Grand Master responded : —

From time immemorial it has been the custom of the Ancient and Honorable Fraternity of Free and Accepted Masons, when requested so to do, to lay, with ancient forms, the corner-stones of buildings to be erected for the worship of God, for charitable objects, for the purposes of the administration of justice and free government, and to consecrate such public monuments as are of patriotic and common interest to the citizens of the Commonwealth.

This Monument, therefore, we may consecrate in accordance with our law, and thus, while testifying our respect for the City of Boston, and our appreciation of the patriotic dead whose released spirits, we believe, now hover near, we shall proceed in accordance with ancient usage.

And as the first duty of Masons, in any undertaking, is to invoke the blessing of the Great Architect upon their work, we will now unite with our Grand Chaplain in an address to the Throne of Grace.

INTRODUCTORY PRAYER BY W. REV. JOSHUA YOUNG, GRAND CHAPLAIN.

O Thou, most high, most holy, we confess Thy greatness and Thy power.

We hail this auspicious day, — day of liberty, day of manifold memories of loyal and heroic deeds and deaths.

Now that we are about to dedicate this Monument, erected to commemorate the patriotic dead, we invoke Thy favor on the services and ceremonies of this hour.

Except the Lord build the house, they labor in vain that build it. We sought Thy blessing when the foundation was laid; be with us now, O our God, and accept and establish the work of our hands; and may this structure stand complete, a grateful and affecting memorial throughout all generations.

Thine is the kingdom, and the power, and the glory, forever and ever. Amen.

After the use of the Square, Level, and Plumb, according to ancient form, the Grand Master, striking the Monument three times with the gavel, said: —

Well made — well proved — true and trusty. This undertaking has been conducted and completed by the Craftsmen according to the grand plan, in Peace, Harmony, and Brotherly Love.

The Deputy Grand Master received from the Grand Marshal the vessel of Corn, and, pouring the Corn, said: —

May the health of the community which has executed this undertaking be preserved, and may the Supreme Grand Architect bless and prosper its labors.

The Grand Marshal presented the Cup of Wine to the Senior Grand Warden, who poured the Wine, saying: —

May plenty be vouchsafed to the people of this ancient city, and may the blessing of the Bounteous Giver of all things attend all its philanthropic and patriotic undertakings.

The Grand Marshal presented the Cup of Oil to the Junior Grand Warden, who poured the Oil, saying: —

May the Supreme Ruler of the World preserve this people in peace, and grant to them the enjoyment of every blessing.

The W. Rev. ALONZO H. QUINT, D.D., Grand Chaplain, offered the following invocation and prayer of consecration: —

INVOCATION.

May Corn, Wine, and Oil, and all the necessaries of life, abound among men throughout the world; and that this structure may long remain in the Beauty and Strength of the Brotherly Love for the departed to whose memory it is now to be consecrated, let us pray.

PRAYER OF CONSECRATION.

Almighty God, who rulest and commandest all things, we present ourselves before Thee to offer the sacrifice of praise and thanksgiving for that Thou heardest us when we called in our trouble, and didst not cast out our prayer which we made to Thee in our great distress; that Thou didst mercifully look upon us and command a deliverance; for which we do now give all praise and glory to Thy holy name.

We bless Thee, who makest wars to cease, that the bugle-call is heard no more, that the battle-smoke has lifted, that the clash of sabres has ceased, and the roar of guns is hushed.

Now, O Lord, from the ocean which washes the Eastern shores of North and South alike, to the ocean which washes our Western cliffs, make us one people in heart and spirit. Preserve and honor the flag which floats over this undivided land. Under it, grant, Thou Ruler of nations, that this whole people may live in peace, harmony, and brotherly love; and that this nation, purified by the trial of fire which Thou didst see was necessary, may stand before Thee in beauty and strength.

We thank Thee that Thou didst keep fresh in the heart of this grateful city the memory of its heroes, and that, therefore, it would build into stone, so that all men might see, their honor for the dead.

We bless Thee that Thou didst give this pictured beauty to the artist's thought and this wondrous skill to the artist's hand.

Gladly do we remember before Thee that these foundations were laid in no spirit to perpetuate remembrance of fratricidal strife or of triumph over men, but were laid to honor the memory of patriotic devotion to the flag of our whole country, and, to that end, of brave self-sacrifice, even unto death.

We praise Thee that by the achievements of such men Thou didst reëstablish our National Union; didst proclaim liberty throughout the land; didst confirm the Constitution which our fathers wrote.

And now, O God, to remember these things, and these men, and for those who builded this Monument in honor of the men who builded anew a nation, have we come to consecrate this stone.

Well made, well proved, builded according to Thine eternal laws, Great Architect of the Universe, approve it, we beseech Thee.

Bless this stone, O heavenly Father —

In honor of mothers who bade their sons do brave deeds:

In honor of wives who wept for the husbands who should never come home again:

In honor of children whose heritage is their fallen father's heroic name:

In honor of men and women who ministered to the hurt and the dying:

But chiefly, O God, in honor of men who counted not their lives dear when their country needed them; of those alike who sleep beside the dust of their kindred, or under the salt sea, or in nameless graves, where only Thine angels stand sentinels till the reveille of the resurrection morning.

Preserve it, we pray, in the years to come; in heat and cold, in snows and rains, in seed-times and harvests. Let it endure, that the men who see it, in the coming generations, may be inspired to know that honor is more than wealth, right is more than peace, and heroic death more than life.

These praises do we render Thee, and these petitions do we offer Thee, in the name of Him who passed through his Gethsemane and suffered upon Calvary. Amen.

The Grand Master made the following address: —

ADDRESS OF THE GRAND MASTER, PERCIVAL LOWELL EVERETT.

The ancient society of Freemasons, locally represented by the Grand Lodge administering its affairs within the territorial jurisdiction of the Commonwealth, in conformity to the teachings of its own history and traditions, and in unison with all ranks and orders of citizens, appears to-day, at the request of the municipal authorities of the capital city, to participate in, and, if possible, to heighten the impressive services of this commemoration. The guild or craft of Freemasons is historically known, not only by its age, but by its distinctive character and qualities, by its nearly all-pervading reach through the various races and forms of civilization, and its connection at all times with the conditions of the civil and social fabric. In the early periods of European society its members were educated and practical constructors, builders of the grand cathedrals and other structures whose massive proportions and architectural fitness still remain to mark the skill in art of those who laid their foundations and raised them to shapes of beauty and grace. Under the influences of time and the general progress and elevation of society, the constructive or operative character of the Masons as builders was so far modified that they became a philosophical, charitable, and social body, whose office was not the building of a physical structure, but the grander edifice of human character.

The practice of building — the exercise of the constructive arts upon those edifices and creations of their skill which were intimately connected, sometimes with religious worship and instruction, and sometimes with the more general intellectual, moral, and social advancement of the people — naturally led our ancestors in operative Masonry into those careful conservatisms of habit, thought, and feeling which became organic in the structure of their society. They thus early learned to do their work so that it should last, — to build even against time itself. It would seem to have been indeed a prime necessity that the imposing structures which had been reared at such a lavish expenditure of thought, of money, and of labor, should not be subject to the obvious perils of revolutionary or turbulent social conditions, to the vicissitudes of a shifting or inconstant government, or to the operation of arbitrary or unequal laws. If these lofty temples were to live out their long day of glory, they must be brooded under the serene and steady influences of a settled and permanent system of government and law. The transition, then, of our early brethren from the practical or operative to a philosophic mode of existence and exercise, though a gradual, was an easy one. They became in like degree — and certainly not without the consenting will of all others interested in the erection and maintenance of a true government — *builders* of the State — constructors of the fabric of society. As in the practice of their operative art they had been led to aim at permanence, so, in the higher construction of a Commonwealth, would they perhaps more readily learn to broaden the foundations and more truly to adjust the proportions of the superstructure of government. For here was the temple in which should be enshrined all human hopes and interests, — everything pertaining to man which could be entrusted to law and civil guardianship, or be promoted by social regulations. The brethren recognized the value of *stability*, of *certainty* in the direction of human affairs, as in that of natural forces. They acquired the wisdom of adherence to settled ways and methods of administration, and of changing slowly. These were lessons of their own organization, and were applied to the structure or system of civil government. Hence, and almost by organic necessity, they came to regard *loyalty* as a principle, — or the idea of entire devotion to the existing government, — as one of the corner-stones of the Masonic structure, and to esteem the fostering care and providence of the *State*, the aspirations of its people for a regulated freedom, the earnest struggle and endeavor of good men for public advancement and development, the austere glory of arms and the serener glory of arts, as subjects nearest the practical concern and duty of the citizen. It was enough for them to consider that, through the instrumentality of a rightly constituted State, as by a divine ordination, there would be most surely attained the largest individual liberty consistent with the general good, the coördination of personal and public obligations with personal and public rights, the most expansive freedom of opinion, and consequently the most generous toleration, and that to these would be added the largest opportunities for the development of all the faculties of manhood and the security of personal happiness.

To be loyal, therefore, to the State, as in the best sense, a *divine* constitution, was simply to be faithful to God. In both instances the allegiance involved the offering of personal service and property, and of life itself. Each constituent member, upon whom rested the obligations, and to whom was pledged the protection of the State, was to serve its interests as for his chiefest good, and alike for life or death. It was no servile obligation, no mere subjection of the weak to the strong, like the slavery of the feudal investiture, but the devotion of a free and interested manhood. The principle of loyalty was subject to all human vicissitudes, but in proportion to its growth and vigor in the ranks of the governed would be the asserting, the aggressive, as well as the defensive power of the government, — its strength for war and peace. And it may be justly said that through the entire era of modern history a constant and unvarying subjection or devotion to the State and government, under whatsoever sky it has held its Lodge, has never been wanting to the Masonic Body.

The part taken by the fraternity in the establishment of our American State in the initiation and accomplishment of the Revolution, the adoption of the Constitution, and the organization of the Federal government, is doubtless known to most of those who listen to me. Our brethren, at once depressed and aroused by political wrongs, suffered by them in common with their fellow-citizens, as colonial subjects of Great Britain, were among the first to feel the sharp promptings of resistance, and to be inflamed by the sacred fires of revolt. It was, perhaps, more notable that they should array themselves in the posture of revolution against the existing government, and assume the perils of the position, since, as subordinates of the dominant Masonic authority of the mother-country, they had suffered no Masonic wrongs or oppressions, but had ever maintained the closest and most serene relations of fraternity with their English brethren. Nevertheless, the principle of loyalty, leading in this exceptional instance, although, by the same logical deductions, to the *overthrow* rather than to the *preservation* of a government whose functions and uses had oppressed instead of serving the people, induced our illustrious brothers, Washington, Franklin, Otis, Warren, Revere, and their associates, to cast their lives into the scale of a new and assuredly doubtful cause. The revolutionary and constitutional fathers, who, through the fires and hardships of the eight years' struggle in arms, and the scarcely less arduous subsequent struggle for the civil results of the contest, were in large numbers attached to the fraternity, upholding its organization, ritual, and ceremonies, even through the most strenuous campaigns of the war.

It may not become the proprieties of the occasion to rehearse the special merits, the peculiar instances of devotion to the country, of distinguished Masons, or to consider in detail the services of the entire fraternity, but I may be indulged in this general allusion to their relation to the inception and prosecution of the revolutionary cause.

From the date of the full triumph of that immortal cause, and the establishment of the Federal system as its grand effect, until the present hour, the members of our fraternity have been identified with all the highest interests and aims of the National and State administrations. Knowing, as a society, neither creed nor dogma in politics or religion, they have contributed, within the capacity of their numbers and influence, to the support and maintenance of the institutions of religion, of philanthropy, of science, and of art. They have interwoven into the fabric of general society — they have incorporated into the very structure of the Commonwealth — the practical doctrines and maxims by which a people, by the forces of organization, have risen to the stature of a well-established State. Often working in the ranks of the humblest service, they have also often illustrated the dignity and elevation of the highest stations. Neither their lofty services nor their lowly duties have been rendered simply because, while they were Masons, they were also citizens, and therefore bound by the commonest ties of mere citizenship to a general allegiance, but because, as Masons, they were individually held by the peculiar force of their Masonic obligation to a special allegiance. The duties and obligations of citizenship thus professed and thus discharged have, therefore, been *functional* with the Craft, — the result of its philosophy and its precepts, — the clear and indisputable issue of its practical teachings in the civic life. In no strain of boasting or self-gratulation, and surely with no depreciation of the good works and the good spirit of the masses of patriotic men who were never linked with us in the bonds of this peculiar brotherhood, I simply assert the truth of History when I declare that the Freemasons of this Commonwealth have never failed in any hour of peace or war in the devotion of life, and all that life holds most dear, to the welfare of the Nation and the State, to the glory of their arms and the happiness of their people. A lesser service they could not have rendered and kept the faith as true and honorable members of the institution.

When, therefore, the great revolt, the suppression of which finds an opportunity for this day's service; the uprising of a section against the nation; the conspiracy of a part against the whole, became manifest to the startled sense of those whose allegiance to a wholesome and beneficent government had never faltered or doubted; and when, in support of that revolt, no oppressions or legitimate causes of revolution could be averred, it was but natural and logical that the conservatism of Masonry should instantly meet, and with corresponding force, any armed resistance to those authorities, which, for the time, represented the divine ordination of government.

Through the long agony from Sumter to Appomattox, the members of the Craft, mingling with their patriotic comrades of every rank and order of citizenship, both by birth and adoption, on the land and on the sea, under the glittering insignia of official commission and the humbler badge of enlistment in the ranks, with sword, musket, and spade, with all implements of offence and defence, with high, heroic hearts, more sturdy than sword or shield, achieving the arduous honors of victory, breasting the waves of defeat and repulse, welcoming the tortures of hospital and prison, bore up the banners of the Union, bringing the costly drain of their vital blood, the vigor of youth and manly strength, and the last feeble effort of declining age, as free gifts of the American citizen-soldier upon the nation's altar, until the scarred and tattered ensigns waved in triumph over the restored and ransomed land. They counted the joys of home, the studies, profits, and employments of peace, as nothing in the contemplation of the patriot citizen when set against the stern but ennobling duties of the hour. While they waged the war inexorably for its results, they sought to mitigate its horrors and asperities. They relieved its features of barbarity without imperilling the vigor of its prosecution. As victors they were ready for an instant embrace in manly and fraternal arms of the vanquished brother upon his surrender to the old allegiance. Their glory and honor throughout the memorable contest is, indeed, but the glory and honor of every soldier and sailor who gave or offered his life for the sacred cause.

The drama of war is ended, — the discord of battle and of civil strife has closed, and peace returns with her grateful olives.

You have come to commit to faithful memory the record of the service and the devotion of the native and adopted sons of Boston in the stupendous civil war, with whose grandest triumphs and successes they were so nobly and honorably associated. Upon the altars of these dead heroes of the service by land and by sea, and of their comrades, to whom, although as freely offered, the "last full measure of devotion" was not permitted, the institution which I have the pleasure officially to represent, with thoughtful reverence brings its choicest garlands of honor and gratitude. With the pomp of ancient rite and ceremony, it bestows upon this lofty material symbol of their sacrifice and patriotism its consecration and benediction. Well may the proud city of their love, with the matured grace of a long-meditated affection, in clustering and radiant forms of the sculptor's art, crystallize for the eyes of posterity their life-work and its heroic end. To no period of history has the devotion of life to the cause of country, or to lesser causes, been wanting.

But the subjects of this day's honor went forth to the gage of battle, not to conquer, but to save, and to save even their enemies. They understood all the issues of the controversy, and comprehended all its perils. They well knew what the American system of constitutional government had wrought in less than a century for one race, and what it promises to do for all races. Out of the fires of war and death they rescued that system. Never in the annals of time has been recorded a higher, a nobler consecration. Monuments can scarcely heighten its significance. History, with its stately record of their achievements, the lyric Muse, chanting their praises in immortal song, and sculpture, weaving in its embroidery of beauty and grace their deeds of heroism, are but voices of the universal heart pronouncing the common eulogy. Under the inevitable wastes of time, the Monument you now rear, as one of the columns of their glory, may crumble; but after that vicissitude, the *city*, the *land*, and every *rood* of *enlightened earth* shall bear them witness. Surely no land ever took back into its grateful bosom a treasure like these dead children of the city and nation. Unshrouded as they lie in their unknown sepulchres of valor, they are buried in the heart of the nation. Garnered in the affections of the whole people, they abide in the gratitude of the present, and shall subsist in the reverting memories of all coming generations. Their mouldering bodies have become constituent parts of the ransomed soil; their radiant spirits have been lifted to the incorporeal essence of the renovated government.

For the future of the land of our love there can be no loftier aspiration than that which to-day fills the breast of the ancient fraternity of Masonry, namely, that for this high sacrifice, for the consecration of these heroes of Boston, — these heroes of America, — there must be exacted and received the fullest satisfaction, the most complete resulting equivalents. The land which they saved must be made and kept wholly worth the saving. The authority of the Federal government within its limits, and of the States within theirs, must be clear and exclusive, without conflict or dispute. The tyranny, the selfishness, and the corruptions of party must make way for the return of pure and incorruptible administration through all the avenues of government, in every department and sphere of its operation. Honesty, with her plain rigors, must revisit the soil, and pervade every fibre of the national being. The desolations of the war must disappear, the waste places must be rebuilt, and the sorer wounds of the affections must be healed. All the forces of public and social law and opinion must combine to the issue of a grand *equality* of citizenship, with no subordination under public or legislative decree, of any race or order, of any sect or party. There must be a loyalty, not of external compliance, but of inward affection; a *Union*, not of conforming hands, but of consenting hearts. There must be a return to the loves of the revolutionary days, to the pure glances of those mutual eyes, which, in all sections of the outspread land, shall be blind to every partial interest, and open only to the common cause and the universal good. This full fraternal union of States, this genius of constitutional government, — the faith of the fathers, the hope of the nations, the expectation of mankind, — *this* shall be our grand Republic; *this*, our beloved America. With the dust of her slaughtered sons transmuted into gems of purest lustre around her brow, she will resume her majestic march down the pathway of time.

The Grand Master, addressing the Grand Marshal, said : —

Worshipful Brother Grand Marshal, — You will make proclamation that this Monument has been duly consecrated in accordance with ancient form and usage.

PROCLAMATION BY THE GRAND MARSHAL.

In the name of the Most Worshipful Grand Lodge of the Commonwealth of Massachusetts, I now proclaim that the Monument here erected by the City of Boston, in memory of our patriotic dead, has this day been found square, level, and plumb, true and trusty, and consecrated according to the ancient forms of Masons.

This Proclamation is made from the EAST, the WEST, the SOUTH,—ONCE, (Trumpet) TWICE (Trumpet twice), THRICE (Trumpet thrice). All interested will take due notice thereof.

At the conclusion of the Masonic services, the Band performed "To Thee, O Country," by Julius Eichberg, after which Alderman THOMPSON delivered the Monument to His Honor the Mayor, as follows:—

Mr. Mayor,—The Joint Special Committee of the City Council, who were appointed to have charge of the erection of the Army and Navy Monument, have executed the trust confided to them, and I now have the honor of surrendering to you, as the chief magistrate of the city, this Monument erected to the memory of our Soldiers and Sailors who lost their lives in the late civil war.

The subject of erecting such a Monument was considered by the City Government soon after the termination of the war, and in 1866 a committee was appointed to consider and report upon the expediency of erecting a Monument, and to recommend a suitable location for the same. Subsequently, in accordance with the report of this committee, another committee was appointed to procure plans and estimates for a Monument, to be erected on Boston Common, and before the close of that year the foundation of the present structure was laid. The committee advertised at two different periods for designs, and a number were submitted, some of the most distinguished artists in the country being among the competitors; and it is peculiarly gratifying to know that to Martin Milmore, one of our own citizens, was awarded the honor of moulding into artistic form this memorial of a grateful people. The completed work bears witness to his fitness for the task.

The corner-stone was laid, with appropriate ceremonies, on the 18th of September, 1871, and from that time forward the work has been steadily progressing.

Eleven years have passed since the first steps were taken toward the erection of this Monument.

When the initiatory measures were adopted the smoke of battle had hardly cleared away, and the nation was still reeling under the shock which it had received; but during the past six years, in which the Monument has been approaching completion, the work of reconciliation has steadily gone on, and, as we assemble to-day, we realize that the labors and sacrifices of those to whose memory we are here to do honor were not in vain. We meet as citizens of a great country, whose sectional differences have been allayed, and who have joined hands once more in fraternal intercourse.

We rejoice to welcome those who have come to join us in paying this tribute to the revered memory of their comrades who gave their lives to their country; and we as gladly extend the right hand of friendship to all those who separated from us in that civil strife, but who have since renewed their pledge of allegiance to our glorious Union, now made " more perfect " by the original inherent cause of difference being entirely and forever removed.

We erected this Monument, sir, not to commemorate the bitter conflict, nor to celebrate our triumph in the fratricidal struggle, but to testify our admiration for that stern devotion to duty and to the cause of freedom which led the men of Boston, true to the traditions of their fathers, to offer up their lives on the altar of their country.

Their graves are scattered from the Atlantic to the Gulf; they sleep beneath the palmetto and the pine; but a grateful city keeps their memory green, and they live forever in the hearts of their countrymen.

In the language of Gov. Andrew, the great War Governor of this Commonwealth: —

> The dead are already immortal. May the solemn dedication of the Monument reared to the men of Boston who fell for their country, renew the profound impressions of gratitude and of duty which belong to the recollection of their career, and may the column which bears their names stand a mute witness to a thousand generations of the beauty and triumph of virtue.

We have selected for the performance of this grateful duty the two hundred and forty-seventh anniversary of our city's birth, of that historic day, when our ancestors, moving from the northern bank of the Charles, settled here, and gave to this place, from their affection to their mother-country, the English name of Boston. This is also the ninetieth anniversary of that no less eventful day when the Constitution of the United States was unanimously ratified in convention, and was officially promulgated by Washington to the old thirteen States for their adoption; and later, within the recollections of all of us, of that day of Antietam, of that terrible battle that brought sorrow and desolation to the homes of so many here, and in this immediate vicinity; and I am reminded that among our distinguished guests, who have come here to participate with us in these dedicatory services, is the Hero of that day, Gen. George B. McClellan.

Impressed by these hallowed associations, we now unveil this Monument, and present it formally to you, sir, that you may receive it under your official protection, to be preserved and cherished by you and your successors in office as a becoming memorial of this eventful era.

The Monument bears upon its face the following classic inscription, prepared by President Eliot, of Harvard University, that venerable institution of learning, which has reared so many illustrious men, who have in peace and in war rendered eminent service : —

> To the men of Boston
> who died for their country
> on land and sea in the war
> which kept the Union whole
> destroyed slavery
> and maintained the Constitution
> the grateful City
> has built this monument
> that their example may speak
> to coming generations

It bears on the cap of its solid and graceful column an imposing statue representing America. Her head is encircled by thirteen stars, her left hand holds the star-spangled banner, and her right hand, adorned with a wreath of laurel, grasps the sword by which the Flag of the Union is ever to be defended. On the lower part of the column are carved in bold relief, figures representing the North, the South, the East, and the West, appropriately placed, signifying that the country will be sustained in every quarter, under whatever emergency.

At the corners above the base are four other statues: the Soldier and the Sailor, emblematic of the Army and Navy; Peace, with her glad promise of the future; and History, ready to continue her record. In the panels formed by the four sides of the base, bronze bas-reliefs are inserted: (1) "The Departure for the War," representing a regiment marching past the State House, on the steps of which stand Governor Andrew, the members of his staff, and others; (2) "The Return from the War," representing the worn veterans with tattered ensign, being welcomed back by the Governor and the people; (3) "Naval Warfare," representing a monitor bombarding a fort; (4) "The Labors of the Sanitary Commission," representing a hospital and its surroundings.

Emblematic wreaths complete the design.

The Monument faces the South in memory of the olden time when the North and the South stood shoulder to shoulder in achievement of Independence and Union, under which the national power has since extended over the vast prairies and rising cities of the West, even to the Pacific shore.

Boston, holding within her expanded limits, Bunker Hill, on which stands the grandest of our national monuments, and embracing many other historical landmarks, contains also other monuments, erected, like this, to those who have in this generation nobly sacrificed their lives at the urgent call of their country. But the language of all these enduring memorials is the same.

They speak the exalted praise of that Roman virtue which is well known to include manhood, integrity, and valor. May this Monumental Metropolis, over which, sir, it is your fortune to preside, uniting now under one city seal the destinies and glories of several renowned municipalities, be ever sustained and cheered by these surrounding tokens of great examples of the past, and be ever constant and strong in the love, the defence, and the advancement of *our whole country*.

His Honor FREDERICK O. PRINCE responded in the following words: —

Mr. Chairman and Gentlemen of the Committee, and Fellow-Citizens, — It is my pleasing duty to receive, on behalf of the City of Boston, this Monument, dedicated to valor and patriotism.

The inscription upon the south panel proclaims it to be built by a grateful people to commemorate the heroism of the dead, who died for the Constitution and the Union, that their example may speak to coming generations.

Erected for such purposes, it becomes a sacred temple, to be regarded with love and veneration, and protected with pious and tender care.

It is fitting that these solemn ceremonies should be had on this day, the anniversary of the settlement of Boston. It is fitting that an event of such grave importance should mark the commencement of another year of our municipal history. We record in our annals many occurrences which we treasure with patriotic pride; but this occasion and all that is associated with it will be kept among our most cherished recollections.

Many years have gone by since the patriotic dead have been laid in their honored graves; but let it not be supposed that the delay in erecting this memorial comes from neglect or indifference on our part. Early action was taken by the city for a cenotaph to our martyrs. In 1866 the municipal government, inspired by the patriotism of its excellent magistrate, Frederick W. Lincoln, "appointed a committee to take into consideration the expediency of erecting a Monument in some prominent place in this city to commemorate the fallen heroes who aided in putting down the Southern rebellion, and in sustaining the Constitution and the union of the States."

In their report, made April 16, 1866, the committee recommended the building of a memorial edifice; but, differences of opinion obtaining as to plans, the matter was delayed until an agreement could be reached. In 1870 the design of the beautiful structure before you by the accomplished artist, Martin Milmore, Esq., was adopted by the government, and the work immediately commenced. The corner-stone was laid by His Honor Mayor

Gaston, on September 17, 1871, with appropriate ceremonies; but, the details of the plan being elaborate, years were required for the completion of the structure.

It now stands before you, finished and complete. This debt of gratitude to the heroic dead has to-day been paid.

Perhaps it is fortunate that this Monument was not sooner erected. The lapse of time has permitted the rankling passions and animosities engendered by war to subside, and those kindly feelings to obtain which should exist between those who speak the same language, obey the same government, follow the same flag, and share the same destiny. If we had assembled to dedicate this structure at an earlier date, all would not have done so with the same satisfaction and delight they feel this day. There would not then have been, as now, peace, harmony, and loyal attachment to the Union everywhere throughout our country; for such was not possible until all the States had secured equal constitutional rights, and these have only been obtained since the administration of the government was controlled by the present National Executive.

Long may this structure stand undisturbed by man and the elements. May centuries outnumbering those that look down from the pyramids roll on and find the statue of America beholding, as now, from yonder shaft, over all our vast domain, a free, happy, prosperous, and united people.

It has been said, that if one had but an hour to live, that hour should be given to his country. We may believe that the dead we commemorate to-day recognized to the fullest this sentiment. We may believe that they felt with the Roman poet, —

Dulce et decorum est pro patriâ mori.

No other motive but patriotism, this highest of duties, could have led them to the dreadful fields of civil strife. Be it remembered that when they went forth they were not mercenaries. They were not in the technical sense, *soldiers*. They were not accustomed to war. They were not trained to arms. They were not of the class, which so often appears in history, — marching to the drums of social war, — men of desperate fortunes with nothing to lose and everything to gain in civil convulsions. They were useful citizens, engaged in peaceful pursuits; in those labors and toils which develop the resources and augment the wealth of the country. They were impelled by no love of military glory, by no vulgar ambition for martial distinction. Patriotism, and patriotism alone, prompted their action. They believed the Union was endangered. They believed the Constitution which makes us one people was imperilled. They believed the liberties we enjoy under the Union and the Constitution were threatened, and, hearing only the call of the nation in its hour of anguish, — forgetful of every thought of personal safety, and every consideration of personal advantage, — marched to the battle-field; and they marched, not with the slow pace of the unwilling and reluctant, but at the charging step of the loyal and the brave, who die for a cause.

How great were the sacrifices of our immortal dead! They forsook home and all its endearments. They parted from wives and children. They left friends and all the enjoyments we have under free institutions. They endured the labors, perils, and sufferings of war, and crowned the sacrifice by the surrender of life itself.

Such patriotism should not be forgotten. The nation benefited by such services and saved by such devotion should keep her heroes in perpetual remembrance.

Rightly, therefore, have our citizens invoked the assistance of art to rear this commemorating column, that our appreciation of their noble deeds and our gratitude for the blessings we enjoy through their sacrifices may be fitly expressed.

But this structure is not needed for the dead. They who have fallen require no monument to perpetuate their deeds. They may say with the Grecian hero — these need not be recited, for all have seen them: —

> Nec memoranda tamen vobis mea facta — Vidistis enim!

Their deeds are a Union restored — a Constitution saved — a Nationality preserved!

If, then, you seek their monument, look around.

The chief object of this admonishing sculpture, as the inscription tells us, is to impress coming generations with the example of the patriotic dead, and animate those who shall come after us and occupy the places we now occupy with similar sentiments of valor, honor, love of country, and devotion to duty.

May then all those who shall come here and behold this sacred pile, may especially the young men, who are the hope of the country, feel and appreciate as they should the associations and suggestions of its solemn presence. And as often as they contemplate the artistic beauty here revealed, as they look upon the majestic statue crowning the column, as they study the patriotic emblems which decorate it, as they gaze upon the tablet which pictures the unreturning brave departing for the battle-field with the benediction of the sainted Andrew,— let us hope that sometimes the shadows of our martyrs will appear to their entranced vision, in transfiguration, assuring them of the glory which rewards heroic deeds, and exhorting them to renewed vows of patriotism and loyalty.

Such are the objects and such the uses of this structure. Who is there of the North, of the South, of the East, or the West, that cannot join with us to-day with heartfelt sympathy in the services of this occasion?

The City of Boston does not erect a Monument to perpetuate strife, and that saddest of strifes, civil war. She does not seek by the eloquence of sculptured stone and bronze to keep alive sectional animosity and acrimony; to keep in remembrance fraternal discord; to remind the gazer of fields red with the blood of countrymen; of victories over the descendants of sires who fought side by side under Washington for the establishment of American independence.

If such had been the purpose of our citizens, it would have been better to have left the granite of this structure unquarried, and the components of this speaking bronze undisturbed in their mines. If the Monument is to commemorate triumphs and victories obtained in civil war, it would have been better to have built it of unenduring wood, like the trophies of the Greeks, so that it might perish and be forgotten with the passions and resentments awakened by the contest. If we had proposed to rear a perpetual record of dissensions which separated American citizens, in the unnatural contest, we should not have asked the presence on this occasion of distinguished guests from the South, nor invited them to unite in our solemn services.

Let the greetings they have this day received, let the memory of the touching scenes and reconciling hospitality of the 17th June, 1875, assure our countrymen that no unkindly feelings are cherished here.

If the commemorated dead could arise and speak to those they have met in battle, their words would not be words of anger, but of peace and good-will. Why, then, should it be otherwise with the living?

The genius of the artist has with great felicity appropriately placed the statue of Peace looking to the *South*. Let us hope that the inspiration which directed his hand was prophetic; that it is an assurance that the past is forgotten; that there are to be no irritating or disturbing memories; that the South, when it looks to the North, shall see, not the sword of victory, but the fraternal hand grasping the olive-branch of reconciliation and friendship.

We should not forget that we have here the brave comrades of our honored dead, the surviving heroes of a hundred battles. I envy them the satisfaction they must feel from the conviction of the great services they have rendered their country,— no, not envy, *non invideo, miror magis;* for I would not pluck a single leaf from their garlands of fame. Long may they live to enjoy the gratitude of the Republic and the glory they have won. And may their honorable wounds and broken health receive what has been too long delayed, the nursing care and support of a Soldiers' Home.

It was the prayer of the great defender of the Constitution that " when his eyes were turned to behold for the last time the sun in heaven, he might not see him shining on the broken and dishonored fragments of a once glorious Union; on States dissevered, discordant, belligerent." He was more fortunate than we have been, for he was spared the agony of our civil contention. But we may thank God — and the dead we commemorate, and these their surviving companions in honor — that we have been permitted to see, ere we are called hence, a restored Union, and an undivided country enjoying all the blessings of liberty and peace. Not the terrible peace made by the devastation and solitude created by war, nor that counterfeit peace which results from a mere cessation of arms; but the true and lasting peace which comes from the restoration of fraternal feelings, the return of mutual good-will and common attachment to our glorious institutions.

I will not detain you longer from the orator of the day, the Hon. Charles Devens, whom I now introduce to you.

The Honorable CHARLES DEVENS, Orator of the Day, then delivered the following address : —

ADDRESS OF HON. CHARLES DEVENS.

Mr. Mayor, Fellow-Citizens, and Comrades, — On the anniversary of a day thrice memorable, as that of the first settlement of this town in 1630; as that of the adoption of the Constitution of the United States in 1789; as that of a great battle fought for the Union on the soil of Maryland in 1862 (the victorious commander in which is to-day among our most honored and illustrious guests), we have assembled to dedicate this Monument to the memory of the brave who fell in that great conflict, which, commencing for the unity of the government, broadened and deepened into one for the equal rights of all men. Before we part, some words should be spoken seeking to express, however inadequately, our gratitude to those to whom it is devoted. Yet our ceremonial will be but vain and empty if its outward acts are not the expressions of feelings deeper than either acts or words. Its true dedication is to be found in the emotions which have been kindled by the occasion itself, and to which every heart has yielded. Here in this city, the capital of Massachusetts, a State from which more than sixty gallant regiments were sent to the field under the inspiration of her illustrious Governor, who now himself sleeps with those whom he sent forth to battle, we seek to surrender by this solemn act, from the age that is passing to the ages that are coming, for eternal memory and honor, the just fame of those who have died for the Union.

This is no Monument to the glories of war. While

great changes for good have been wrought, and great steps taken toward liberty and civilization, by the convulsive energies exhibited in wars, these are but exceptions to the great rule that, of all the causes which have degraded nations, opposed human progress, and oppressed industry, war has been one of the worst. If this were its object, it were better far that the stones which compose it had slumbered in their native quarries. No pomp and circumstance, no waving of banners, no dancing of plumes, can lend to war true dignity. This is to be found alone in a great and noble cause.

Nor is this a Monument to valor only. There is something honorable in the true soldier, who, resolutely hazarding life, stands for the flag he follows; but there is that which is higher and nobler here. Among the finest monuments of Europe is that which is found in the beautiful valley of Lucerne, to the memory of the Swiss Guard who fell around Louis XVI., when the furious mob had stormed his palace. Placed in a niche of the limestone cliff, of which it forms a part, a lion pierced with a spear still holds in his death-grip the shield on which are carved the arms of the Bourbon. Few works of art are more majestic, or more fully show the hand of the master. It is courage only that it honors, and you wonder at the power which has so ennobled and dignified it, when the great idea of patriotism was wanting. The Swiss, whom it commemorates, simply did bravely the work which they had contracted to do, when the subjects of the king, whose bread they had eaten, and whose wine they had drank, deserted him. The men whom we commemorate were brave as these, yet their place in history is not with them. It is with the soldiers of liberty, who have fallen a willing sacrifice for country with patriotic devotion. It is with the Swiss, who, at Sempach or Morgarten, in defence of their own freedom, broke the power of the House of Austria, and not with the mercenaries whom they have sent to fight the battles of Europe.

The sentiment of this Monument is patriotism. The men whom it honors were soldiers, courageous to the death; but it is their cause which sets them apart, for just honor and commendation, among the millions who have laid down their lives upon the battle-field. Patriotism such as theirs is the highest of civic virtues, the noblest form of heroism. Those who perilled their lives in obedience to its promptings could gain no more than those who remained at home in inglorious ease; and yet they laid aside their hopes of comfort, to die for us. That the government they had lived under might be preserved, that the just and equal rights of all men might be maintained, they encountered disease, danger, and death, in all the horrid forms in which they present themselves to every one who takes his place in the ranks of an army, with the solemn belief that in no other way could they discharge the obligation imposed upon them by their birthright as citizens of a free country. Whatever might be its difficulties and dangers, their path was so clearly indicated that they deemed they could not err in following it. When they fought and fell they could not know but that their efforts would be in vain, and the great flag, the symbol of our united sovereignty, be rent asunder; but they were ready to risk all, and to dare all, in the effort to deserve success.

They were animated by no fierce fire of ambition; no desire to exalt themselves; no expectation of attaining those rewards which are gained by great chieftains. They had no such hopes. They knew well that all the honor they could obtain was that general meed of praise awarded to all who serve faithfully, but which would not separate them from others who had been brave and true. No doubt, as the blood of youth was high in their veins, they looked forward, in some instances, to the stern joy of the conflict; but beyond and above its tempest, fire, and smoke, they beheld and strove for the great objects of the contest.

To-day they have seemed to come again as when they moved out in serried lines, with the flag which they went to defend waving above their heads. Again we have seemed to see them, their faces lighted with patriotic enthusiasm, and we have recalled the varied scenes of their stern and manly service, which was to end in a soldier's death for the country to which they had devoted themselves; in each and every fortune patient and determined, staining their cause with no weakness or cowardice, dishonoring it by no baseness or cruelty.

When we reflect how little our system of education is calculated to adapt men to the restraints of military service, how inconsistent its largeness and freedom is with that stern control which necessarily marks a system intended to give a single mind the power which is embodied in thousands of men, we may well wonder at the ready submission which was always given to its exactions. To some the possession of marked military qualities, adapting them to control others, gave prominence; to some mere accidents of time or circumstance may have given high commands, while others, not less worthy, filled only their places, and did their duty in the ranks. But those who led must often have felt that their highest desire should be to be worthy of the devotion of those who followed. The distinctions necessary to discipline have long since passed away. Side by side, on fields bought by their blood, "no useless coffins around their breasts," but wrapped in the blanket which is the soldier's martial shroud, awaiting the coming of the Eternal Day, they rest together.

What matter is it while men have given of their utmost in intellect, strength, and courage, and of their blood to the last drop, whether they fell with the stars of the general, the eagles of the colonel, on their shoulders, or in the simple jacket of the private? Wherever "on fame's eternal camping-ground their silent tents are spread," in the tangled wildwood, in the stately cemetery, or in nameless graves, not even marked by the word "unknown," the earth that bears them dead bears not alive more true or noble men. To-day we remember them all, without regard to rank or race, seeking to honor those whom we cannot by name identify.

If we do not commend patriotism such as these men exhibited, to whom are we to turn in the hour of danger which may come to those who are to succeed us, as it did to ourselves? Lessons such as they have given are not to be idly neglected when the time is gone when their services have ceased to be of immediate value. We shall not need to go to Marathon and Platea for examples, whose brethren have shed their blood on fields as fiercely contested as those; and it would be idle to go anywhere for examples, unless, in rendering homage to the valor and patriotism displayed by our brethren, we seek to reconsecrate ourselves to the same virtues. Every instinct of justice calls upon us for the appropriate meed of praise, every suggestion of wisdom counsels that we omit no opportunity to instil into others the admiration with which their deeds are regarded. The fables of romance, which, in some form, each nation of Europe has, that in great emergencies their illustrious chiefs will return again to rescue them, are not altogether myths. To each people that loves bravery and patriotism come again in their hour of trial the old heroic souls, although the form and garb they wear is of their present age and time.

The time for natural tears has passed. To every heart the years have brought their new store of joys and sorrows, since these men made their great sacrifice for country. The structure that we have reared stands to honor, and not to mourn, the dead. So shall it stand when we in our turn are gone, to teach its lesson of duty nobly done, at the expense of life itself, to those who are in turn to take upon themselves the duties of life.

Those whose names it honors were known and loved by us, and are not to be recalled but with that manly sorrow born of respect and love. There are those also to whom they were even nearer and dearer than to us, who knew them as comrades, whose homes are forever darkened by the absence of the light of affection which their presence shed around them. But the age comes swiftly on which is to know them only by their deeds. We commend them to the grave and impartial tribunal of history as patriotic and devoted citizens; we invoke the considerate judgment of the world upon the justice of their cause; we renew and reiterate the assertion that there was a solemn duty laid upon them by their time, their place, their country, and that such duty they met and performed. To them, as to the Spartans who fell around their king in stern defence of the liberties of Greece, changing but the name of the battle-field, apply the words which Simonides uttered: —

> Of those who at Thermopylæ were slain,
> Glorious the doom and beautiful the lot,
> Their tomb an altar, men from tears refrain,
> Honor and praise, but mourn them not.

Although this Monument may often be passed as a thing of custom, although the lesson which it teaches may seem to be forgotten, yet in the hour of trial, if it is to come to others as it came to us, it will be freshly remembered. As in the Roman story which tells of Hannibal, the mightiest enemy Rome ever knew, it is related that his father, Hamilcar, himself a chieftain and a warrior, whose renown has been eclipsed by that of his greater son, brought him when a child of nine years old into the Temple of the Gods, that he might lift his little hands to swear eternal hostility to the tyranny of

Rome: so shall those who succeed us come here to swear hostility, not to one grasping power only, but to every tyranny that would enslave the body or enchain the mind of man, and eternal devotion to the great principles of civil and religious liberty.

Nor is this Monument, while it asserts our belief in the fidelity of these men, in any sense unkind or ungenerous towards those with whom they were engaged in deadly strife. It bears no words of boasting or unseemly exultation, and the assertion of the justice of their cause, though firmly made, is yet not made in any harsh or controversial spirit. We recognize fully that those with whom they warred were our countrymen; we know their valor and determination; we know that no foot of ground was yielded to us until to hold it became impossible, and that they resisted until men and means utterly and hopelessly failed. Whatever we may think of their cause, that as a people they believed in it cannot fairly be questioned. Men do not sacrifice life and property without stint or measure except in the faith that they are right. Upon individuals we may charge unreasonable temper, intolerance, passion, and the promptings of a selfish and ill-regulated ambition; but the whole body of a people do not act from motives thus personal, and have a right to have their bravery and sincerity admitted, even if more cannot be conceded.

The great conflict was fought out and the victory won which has established forever, if the force of arms can establish anything, that the Republic is one and indivisible, and amid the roar of battle and the clash of arms the institution of slavery, which divided us as a nation, which made of the States two classes diverse and discordant, has passed away. Perhaps, if we had fully known all that it was to cost, both at the North and South, we should have hesitated more than we did before engaging in a strife so deadly and terrible. Yet, as we consider all the woes which must have followed the dismemberment of the Union, as we contemplate the vast gain for peace, freedom, and equality by the emancipation of the subject race from slavery and the dominant race itself from the corrupting influence of this thraldom, who shall say that we have any right to deplore the past except with mitigated grief? We are yet too near the events through which we were swept upon the bloody currents of the war to appreciate their full extent and magnitude, or all the consequences which are to flow from them. We know already that we enter upon a higher plane of national life, when it is established that there are no exceptions to the great rules of liberty among men, and that each is entitled to the just rewards of his labor and the position to which his talents, ability, and virtue entitle him. As we stand here in memory of our gallant dead, we urge upon all who have contended with them to unite with us in the effort to make of our new and regenerated government, purified by the fires of our civil conflict, a Republic more noble and more august than its founders had dared to hope.

Among all patriotic men there is everywhere an earnest desire that there shall be full peace and reconciliation between the sections of the Union. Whatever may have been former divisions, there is nothing in the events of the past, there is nothing in the present condition of things, which should forbid this. We can stand, firmly and securely stand, upon that which has been definitely settled by the war. Ours was not a mere conflict of dynasties, or of families, like the English wars of the Roses, in which the great Houses of York and Lancaster disputed the English Crown. It was a great elemental conflict, in which two opposite systems of civilization were front to front and face to face. It was necessary that one or the other should conquer, and that it should be settled whether the continent should be all free or all slave. Yet the history of civil wars demonstrates that the widest and saddest differences of religion, the most radical differences as to the form of government, have not prevented firm union when the cause of dissension was obliterated.

Now that it is determined that Union is to exist, it must be rendered one of mutual respect and regard, as well as of mutual interest. Unless this is the case there is no cohesive pressure of either internal or external force strong enough to maintain it. There must have been a party victorious and a party vanquished; but there is no true victory anywhere unless the conclusion is for the interest of each and all. It is not the least of the just claims that the American Revolution has upon the friends of liberty everywhere, that, while it terminated in the dismemberment of the British Empire, it left the English a more free people than they would have been but for its occurrence. It settled for them more firmly the great safeguards of English liberty in the right of the habeas corpus, the trial by jury, and the great doctrine that representation must accompany taxation. We speak of it as the victory of Adams and Jefferson, but it was not less that of Chatham and Burke.

I should deem the war for the Union a failure, I should think the victory won by these men who have died in its defence barren, if it shall not prove in every larger sense won for the South as well as the North; if it shall not be shown that it is better for her that the contest against its rightful authority failed.

It is not to be expected that opinion will be changed by edicts, even when those edicts are maintained by force. The changes of opinion must be gradual, and must be the effect of that time which enables feeling to subside and the judgment to act. Already there are brave and reflecting men who fought against us who do not hesitate to acknowledge that the end was well for them as for us, and who look forward hopefully to better results than could have been expected from a Confederacy which, if it had been founded, would have been at the mercy of each individual State. Nor is there any one bold enough to say, now that the system of slavery is destroyed, he would raise a hand, or lift a finger, to replace it. That the cause for which they have suffered so much will still be dear to those who have fought for it, or with whom it is associated by tender and affectionate recollections of those whom they have loved, who have fallen in its defence, is to be expected. To such sentiments and feelings it is a matter of indifference whether there is defeat or success. They would exist, indeed, even if the reason and judgment should concede the cause to have been unwise. Certainly, we ourselves, had the war for the Union failed, would not the less have believed it just and necessary, nor the less have honored the memory of those engaged in it. When results are accepted cordially, we can ask no more until the softening influences of time have done their work.

On the fields which were ploughed by the fierce artillery the wheat has been dancing fresh and fair in the breezes of the summer that is gone; and as the material evidences of the conflict pass away, so let each feeling of bitterness disappear, as together, both North and South, we strive to render the Republic one whose firm yet genial sway shall protect with just and equal laws each citizen who yields obedience to her power. Asking for ourselves no rights that we do not freely concede to others, demanding no restraints upon others that we do not readily submit to ourselves, yielding a generous obedience to the Constitution in all its parts, both new and old, let us endeavor to lift ourselves to that higher level of patriotism which despises any narrow sectionalism, and rejoices in a nationality broad enough to embrace every section of the Union, and each one of its people, whether high or humble, rich or poor, black or white.

There is no division to-day among the States of the Union such as existed when the Constitution was formed. In each and all the great principles of liberty and equal rights are the same, to be alike respected as the only basis upon which the Government can stand. Whatever may have been the sorrows or the losses of the war, there is no sorrow that cannot find its recompense in the added grandeur and dignity of the whole country.

Comrades: —

It is the last time that we, who have marched under the flag, and been the soldiers of the Union in its mortal struggle, shall gather in such numbers as meet to-day. We are an army to whom can come no recruits. The steady, resistless artillery of time hurls its deadly missiles upon us, and each hour we are fewer and weaker. But, as we stand together thus, as we remember how nobly and bravely life's work was done by these men whom we have sought to commemorate, let us believe that the tie which binds us to them, in a great and holy cause, is not wholly dissolved. Their worldly task is done, their solemn oath, which we took side by side with them, is performed. For us life brings each day its new duties and new responsibilities.

In the classic mythology, which was the religion of the ancient world, it was fabled that the heroes were demi-gods. Raised above the race of man, and yet not so far but their example might be imitated, they served to animate those who yet struggled with their mortal surroundings. So should these, our heroes, while the dust of life's conflict is yet on us, inspire us to loftier purposes and nobler lives. And, as we leave them to their glorious repose, and their pure and noble fame, let us go forth exalted by these hours of communion with them.

Above them, as we depart, we utter the ancient form of words, and yet in no formal way, which conclude the proclamations of the State whose children they were: "God save the Commonwealth of Massachusetts!" And to this we add, with not less of fervor or solemnity, the prayer which was in their hearts, and upon their lips, as they died: "God save the Union of the American States!"

At the close of the oration the audience were dismissed with a benediction by Rev. WARREN H. CUDWORTH.

ILLUMINATIONS AND EVENING CONCERT.

A pleasing feature of the occasion was the illumination of the Monument and fountain in the evening by the calcium lights. Two lights located opposite each other on the margin of the pond were focused on the fountain, and the water was illuminated by white, red, blue, green, yellow, and purple lights in succession.

Five lights were focused on the Monument, two on the south side, and one each on the north, east, and west sides. The effect was very fine, and apparently gave great satisfaction to the immense throng which completely covered the hill and valley immediately surrounding the Monument.

During the illumination a concert was given by the Boston Cadet Band, under the leadership of John C. Mullaly. The following programme was given: —

1. MARCH. "Helmstadt," first time .		*Plaade*
2. OVERTURE. "Crown Diamonds" .		*Auber*
3. CONCERT WALTZ. "Normen"	.	*Strauss*
4. CORNET SOLO. "Brilliante"		*Arban*
Performed by WALTER EMERSON.		
5. GRAND SELECTION. "Dinorah"		. *Meyerbeer*
6. CAPRICE. "La Baladine" .		*Lysberg*
7. POT-POURRI. "Girofle Girofla"	.	*Lecocq*
8. FANTASIE FOR "PICCOLO"		*De Carlo*
Performed by A. DAMM.		
9. POT-POURRI. "Harvard" . .		. *Mullaly*
10. GALOP. "Fairy Queen"		*Sydney Smith*
11. MEDLEY OF NATIONAL AND POPULAR AIRS.		

FINAL PROCEEDINGS.

At a meeting of the Board of Aldermen, held on the 24th of September, 1877, the following orders and resolution were offered by Alderman Francis Thompson, and were severally passed by a unanimous rising vote : —

CITY OF BOSTON.

IN BOARD OF ALDERMEN, Sept. 24, 1877.

Ordered, That the thanks of the City Council be presented to the Hon. CHARLES DEVENS for the very eloquent and patriotic oration delivered by him before the municipal authorities of this city at the dedication of the Army and Navy Monument upon Boston Common, on the 17th day of September, A.D. 1877; and that he be requested to furnish a copy for publication.

Resolved, That the thanks of the City Council are due, and they hereby are tendered, to AUGUSTUS P. MARTIN, his aids and assistants, for the very acceptable and successful formation and management of the military and civic procession on the 17th inst., in honor of the completion of the Army and Navy Monument on Boston Common.

Ordered, That the thanks of the City Council be presented to Commodore FOXHALL A. PARKER, of the United States Navy, for the valuable services and assistance rendered, by his permission, to the Committee of Arrangements at the dedication of the Army and Navy Monument on the 17th inst.; and especially for the escort furnished to the City Government by the Marine Corps and Sailors, which formed so conspicuous a feature in the procession.

At its meeting on the 27th of September the Common Council concurred in the passage of the above orders and resolution, and they were approved by His Honor Mayor Prince on the 29th of September.

www.ingramcontent.com/pod-product-compliance
Lightning Source LLC
Chambersburg PA
CBHW030302170426
43202CB00009B/838